Paul Emmerson

email English

Includes
phrase bank
of useful
expressions

MACMILLAN

Macmillan Education
Between Towns Road, Oxford OX4 3PP
A division of Macmillan Publishers Limited
Companies and representatives throughout the world

ISBN 13: 978-1-4050-1294-2

First published 2004

Designed by Mike Brain Graphic Design Limited
Cover design by Andrew Oliver
Cover image by Getty Royalty Free

The author would like to thank Annie Taylor, Marcia Danby
and Colin Jessop for comments on earlier drafts of this book.

The publishers would like to thank Catherine Kerr-Dineen
and Pete Sharma for their comments, and Celia Bingham for
all her hard work.

Printed and bound in Great Britain by Martins the Printers
Limited, Berwick-on-Tweed.

2008 2007
10 9 8 7 6 5

Contents

To the student

Who is this book for?

Learners of English at intermediate or upper-intermediate level who want to write better emails. Learners studying on their own, or with a teacher.

Why was this book written?

In many English courses writing gets a low priority. Sometimes you do have a chance to practise some writing, but without a focus on emails. That is surprising, because emails are probably the most common type of written communication. *Email English* will give you the help you need to write effective emails.

Perhaps you think that it is not worth spending time on emails. They are informal, written quickly, and no-one minds if you make mistakes. Well, that is true for some emails, for example emails between close friends. But what about an email to someone where you want to make a good impression? Or what about an email where you want to be a bit more careful or more diplomatic than usual? Or what about an email in a professional context? It takes awareness and practice to write in a style that fits the context, and *Email English* has many exercises to help you do this.

How is the book organised?

Email English consists of thirty-two units of language practice and a phrase bank. The language practice covers a wide range of topics and includes a great variety of exercise types, such as practice of key phrases, awareness activities about different styles of writing and practice of general language structures. The phrase bank has useful expressions divided into sections. At the end of the book is an answer key.

How should I use this book?

Look at the contents page and you will see that there are various sections in the book. Start with the 'Introduction' units – you will get an idea of how email writing style is different from the style of a letter. Then complete the 'Basics' section. You will practise and learn common phrases for most typical short emails. After that you can work through the book in sequence, or you might prefer to do the units in another order, for example according to what type of emails you most frequently write.

Use the phrase bank as a reference when you write your own emails. The phrases in each section are presented in the most likely order that you will need them, so you get help with the structure of the email as well as the language.

By the time you finish *Email English* you will be much more confident at writing emails. Your emails will be right for the context: friendly and informal, or simple and direct, or polite and indirect, depending on what is best for the situation. And in general you will be able to express yourself more clearly, you will create a good image, and your writing will be easier to understand. Other people will want to know you better, as a friend or colleague or business partner.

What else can I do to practise writing emails?

Get feedback on the emails that you write in real life: if you know a friend whose English is better than yours, or a native speaker, then ask them to make comments on your writing. Also, study the English in the emails you receive. If you receive a well-written email, remember to look carefully at the language. Build your own phrase book: start your own bank of phrases from ones you have received in an email or ones you have written yourself.

If you want more help with grammar, we recommend *Business Grammar Builder* (Macmillan) by Paul Emmerson, the same author as this book.

General tips

Here are some general tips as a reminder for writing good emails:

- Use a 'subject line' that summarises briefly and clearly the content of the message. Your email may be one of hundreds on the recipient's computer, and you want them to read it when it arrives and then find it again easily in their files.

- Use short, simple sentences. Long sentences are often difficult to read and understand. The most common mistake for learners of English is to translate directly from their own language. Usually the result is a complicated, confusing sentence.

- One subject per email is best. The other person can reply to an email about one thing, delete it, and leave another email in their 'Inbox' that needs more time.

- Be very careful with jokes, irony, personal comments etc. Humour rarely translates well from one culture to another. And if you are angry, wait for 24 hours before you write. Once you press 'Send' you cannot get your email back. It can be seen by anyone and copied and sent round the world. The intimate, informal nature of email makes people write things that they shouldn't. Only write what you would be comfortable saying to the person's face.

- Take a moment to review and edit what you have written. Is the main point clear? Would some pieces of continuous text be better as bullet points or numbered points? Is it clear what action you want the recipient to take? Would you be happy to receive this email? If in doubt, ask a colleague to quickly look through and make comments.

- Don't ignore capital letters, punctuation, spelling, paragraphs, and basic grammar. It might be okay when you are writing to a very close friend, but to everyone else it's an important part of the image that you create. A careless, disorganised email shows the outside world a careless, disorganised mind.

- Use the replies you receive to modify your writing to the same person. If the recipient writes back in a more informal or more formal style, then match that in your future emails to them. If they use particular words or phrases that seem to come from their company culture, or professional area, then consider using those words yourself where they are appropriate.

- Be positive! Look at these words: *activity, agreed, evolving, fast, good question, helpful, join us, mutual, productive, solve, team, together, tools, useful*. Now look at these: *busy, crisis, failure, forget it, hard, I can't, I won't, impossible, never, stupid, unavailable, waste*. The words you use show your attitude to life.

To the teacher

What is *Email English*?

Email English is a book to help your students write better emails. It is aimed at intermediate or upper-intermediate level, and consists of 32 two-page units of language practice covering a very wide range of topics, a phrase bank of useful expressions divided into sections, and an answer key.

Email English includes exercises on email style, but also practises more conventional language areas such as fixed expressions, sentence structure, linking words, prepositions and verb tenses. *Email English* assumes that students already have approximately 'intermediate' level, and exercises are designed to review language at this level rather than present it for the first time. If your students want more help with grammar, we recommend *Business Grammar Builder* (Macmillan) by Paul Emmerson.

Why *Email English*?

Writing gets a low priority in many coursebooks, and very few give a systematic and comprehensive treatment of emails. This is surprising, because emails are by far the most common method of written communication, and writing emails is included in many examinations. Working through *Email English* will make your students much more confident in this area. They will be able to express themselves more clearly, their writing will be easier to understand, and they will be able to pass examination questions based on writing emails with much higher marks.

How can you use *Email English* in class?

Work through units 1–3 of *Email English* in sequence. After that, you can do the units in any order. Encourage your students to use the phrase bank as a reference for when they write their own emails. The phrases in each section are presented in the most likely order that a writer will need them, so the student gets help with the structure of the email as well as the language.

Free writing practice and the *Email English* website

Email English is designed for self-study as well as classroom use, so there is no 'free' writing practice in the book. This is convenient for teachers if you don't have time for a follow-up writing task. But if you do want to set a freer writing activity at the end of a unit, then we have included some suggested tasks on this website: **www.businessenglishonline.net**. There are tasks for both working professionals, and for students in Higher Education who have little experience of the professional world. Encourage your students to write emails using a word processor, then they can go back and change it after they get your comments. Soon they will build up a bank of emails they have written. Also encourage them to bring in any well-written emails they receive, so you can study them in class together. From time to time also remind your students to look again at the 'General tips' on page 5.

Organising a writing task

The first choice that you have is students writing their emails in class or for homework. If students write in class you will be able to go round monitoring and helping. A word limit or time limit will help to focus the activity. As you circulate, note down any points that you think would be of interest to other students as well, and cover them in a short feedback slot with the whole class at the end.

When students finish writing they can hand in their work to you for marking, or work in pairs to improve each other's work, or use their ideas to build up a 'collective best version' on the board. Let's look at each option in more detail:

1 Teacher marks the students' work. You can give explicit correction by underlining and writing in the correct form. Alternatively, you can give guided correction by underlining only, perhaps with a hint in the margin, and asking students to try to correct their work themselves. The most challenging form of correction is to not underline any words, but to write a comment in the margin next to the appropriate line (e.g. 'verb tense', 'preposition', 'word order' or 'formality'). Students then work in pairs in the next class to help each other to respond to your comments. Don't forget to acknowledge good use of language in your feedback – a specific comment in the margin (*Good use of this phrase*), or a more general word of encouragement at the end (*Very well written; A big improvement*).

2 Students work in pairs to correct and improve each other's work. Students learn a lot by correcting errors in other students' work, and it helps them to get into the habit of reviewing and editing. They can also learn positive things from another student's text: fixed expressions, grammar, topic vocabulary, style, other ways to organise ideas etc. Peer correction also helps change the classroom atmosphere from the quiet, heads-down writing task to something more lively and communicative. After students have worked together to check and correct each other's comments, leave time for them to rewrite their emails individually before they finally hand them in to you. A similar idea is when students finish their first individual writing, ask them to leave their emails on the desk in front of them, or stick them up on the board/walls. Then ask them to go round and read all the other emails, looking at the structure, organisation of ideas, and noting down any good phrases that other students used. Then they return to their seats and make any changes that they want to.

3 Collective best version on the board. This method is good in small classes where all the students have been doing the same task and the content of their emails is similar. Go through the email sentence by sentence. Each time begin by asking one or two students to suggest an idea, then the whole class (including you) can comment on, reformulate and improve these ideas. Build up an agreed version bit by bit on the board. Of course, the final words will be different to what any one student originally wrote.

Always consider the idea of repeating a task in a later lesson. The students will use the same instructions and can look briefly at their previous, corrected version before they begin. Then they write the same email again. The importance of repeated practice of this kind is often underestimated by teachers who think it might be boring for students. Students tend to recognise that it helps build fluency in writing. Repeating an email from a previous lesson is also a good 'filler' activity for the end of a lesson.

Finally, an email is something that someone sends to someone else. So look for opportunities in class for students to 'send' emails to each other, and for the recipient to write a reply.

1 Formal or informal?

A **First, read the information about writing emails then match the informal phrases (1–15) with the neutral/formal phrases (a–o).**

Three different writing styles are often identified, although in real life the differences are not so clear:

Formal   This is the style of an old-fashioned letter. Ideas are presented politely and carefully, and there is much use of fixed expressions and long words. The language is impersonal. Grammar and punctuation are important. This style is not common in emails, but you can find it if the subject matter is serious (for example a complaint).

Neutral/   This is the most common style in professional/work emails. The writer and reader
Standard   are both busy, so the language is simple, clear and direct. Sentences are short and there is use of contractions (*I've* for *I have* etc.). The language is more personal. However, the style is not similar to speech – it is too direct.

Informal   This is the most common style for emails between friends. Sometimes the email can be very short or it could include personal news, funny comments etc. This is the style that is closest to speech, so there are everyday words and conversational expressions. The reader will also be more tolerant of bad grammar etc.

Informal	Neutral/Formal
1 What do you need? _d_	a) With regard to … (*or* With reference to)
2 Thanks for the email of 12 Feb. _h_	b) I can assure you that …
3 Sorry, I can't make it. _i_	c) We note from our records that you have not …
4 I'm sorry to tell you that … _n_	d) Please let us know your requirements.
5 I promise … _b_	e) I was wondering if you could …
6 Could you …? _e_	f) We would like to remind you that …
7 You haven't … _c_	g) I look forward to meeting you next week.
8 Don't forget … _f_	h) Thank you for your email received 12 February.
9 I need to … _a_	i) I am afraid I will not be able to attend.
10 Shall I …? _j_	j) Would you like me to …?
11 But … / Also … / So … _o_	k) I would be grateful if you could …
12 Please could you … _k_	l) Please accept our apologies for …
13 I'm sorry for …	m) It is necessary for me to …
14 Re …	n) We regret to advise you that …
15 See you next week. _g_	o) However … / In addition … / Therefore …

Note: with business emails you can mix styles to some extent, but don't mix styles at the two extremes. If in doubt, follow the style of the other person.

B   Rewrite the emails below by substituting the phrases in *italics* with more informal phrases. Section A will help you. Use contractions (e.g. *I'll*) where appropriate.

Email 1

> *I am afraid I will not be able to attend the meeting on Friday.* As *I will* miss the meeting, *I was wondering if you could* send me a copy of the minutes? *I will* write to Anita as well, to *inform* her that *I will not* be there. Once again, *please accept my apologies for* this, and *I can assure you that* I will be at the next meeting.

Sorry I can't make it on Friday.

Email 2

> *Thank you for your email of 25 January* where you *requested assistance* on how to order on-line. *It is necessary for me to* know your a/c number before I can deal with this. *I would be grateful if you could* also provide details of which version of Windows *you are* using.

Email 3

> *With reference to* your order number J891 – we received it this morning, but you *have not* filled in the sections on size and colour. *Please let us know your exact requirements.* These products are selling very well at the moment, and *we regret to advise you that* the medium size is temporarily out of stock. *However, we are* expecting more supplies *in the near future. Would you like me to* email you when they arrive?

C   Match the words of Latin origin in box A with the shorter words in box B.

Box A

1 ~~assistance~~	6 information	11 repair
2 due to	7 obtain/receive	12 request
3 enquire	8 occupation	13 requirements
4 further	9 possess	14 reserve
5 inform	10 provide	15 verify

Box B

a) ask	f) facts	k) ~~help~~ (n)
b) ask for	g) fix (v)	l) job
c) because of	h) get	m) more
d) book (v)	i) give	n) needs (n)
e) check/prove	j) have	o) tell

1 _k_ 2 ____ 3 ____ 4 ____ 5 ____ 6 ____ 7 ____ 8 ____ 9 ____ 10 ____ 11 ____ 12 ____ 13 ____ 14 ____ 15 ____

Note: longer words of Latin origin sound more *formal*, and shorter words sound more *informal*.

2 Missing words and abbreviations

A **Read the information below. Then match the sentences (a–l) to their descriptions.**

Missing out words is common in emails and informal speech. It happens where the people know each other very well and the situation is relaxed and friendly. The meaning is clear from the context so the full grammatical form is not necessary.

a) (That's a) good idea!

b) (Did you) get my last email?

c) (I) think your idea is great.

d) (It) sounds like fun!

e) (I am) looking forward to seeing you.

f) (I'll) speak to you later.

g) Just read (the) email about relocation.

h) Your suggestion (is) good, but needs clarification.

i) (Are you) coming with us on Friday?

j) (I) hope you're well.

k) (It's a) pity we missed you yesterday.

l) Next week (would be) better than this week.

1 The subject 'I' can be left out, especially with mental verbs like *hope, think* etc. ..*c*.. / ....

2 In a question, the subject 'you' and the auxiliary can be left out. .... / ....

3 The subject 'I' and the auxiliary (*be, have, will*) can be left out. .... / ....

4 The words 'That' or 'It' can be left out, often with a form of 'be' as well. .... / .... / ....

5 A form of 'be' can be left out on its own. .... / ....

6 The word 'the' can occasionally be left out. ....

B **Put the missing words back into the email below.**

> *It was a*
> ⟨Great evening, wasn't it! Really enjoyed the meal, and nice to see Mary and Roger again. Had a chance to speak to Lucy yet? Don't worry if you haven't, will be seeing her tomorrow.
>
> About next week – film you suggested sounds great. Been talking to some colleagues at work about it. Not sure about the day, though. Tuesday might be difficult. Perhaps Wednesday better? Let me know.
>
> Going to my parents at weekend – looking forward to it. They live in Chichester. Ever been there?
>
> Sometime soon we need to talk about holiday plans for next summer. Things still a bit uncertain at work. Might be possible to take two weeks off in July, but can't be sure. Three weeks impossible. A pity.
>
> Anyway, got to go now. Hope you're well. See you next week.

C **Match the abbreviations (1–4) with the meanings (a–d).**

1 i.e. (*id est*) ....

2 e.g. (*exempli gratia*) ....

3 NB (*nota bene*) ....

4 PS (*postscript*) ....

a) I am going to give an example.

b) I am going to explain what I mean using different words.

c) I am adding some information at the end that I forgot.

d) I want you to give special attention to this next point.

D **First, read the information about abbreviated forms. Then write out the emails in full.**

In some emails you can find very abbreviated forms. The writer wants to write very quickly and the meaning is clear from the context. There are three techniques:

1 using a letter to stand for a sound ('c' = *see*)
2 making a short form of a common word ('yr' = *your*)
3 writing the first letters of a well-known phrase ('asap' = *as soon as possible*).

Email 1

> Subject: Yr order ref no KD654
> In relation to yr order rec'd today, we cannot supply the qty's you need at this moment. Pls confirm asap if a part-delivery wd be acceptable, with the rest to follow L8R. Rgds, Stefan.

Subject: ...... *Your order reference number KD654* ......

....
....
....
....

Email 2

> Subject: Thx for yr msg
> Re your msg left on my ans machine – yes, I'm free 4 lunch on Wed next wk. Btw, good news about yr interview. Hv 2 work now. CU, Jane.

Subject: ....

....
....
....
....

Email 3

> Subject: Options for Tech Help
> We have a Tech Assistance section on our website, with an extensive list of FAQs. Customers find this v convnt as it is avail 24/7. Otoh, if you need to spk to sb in person, you can call during wkng hours. Bw, Alan.

Subject: ....

....
....
....
....
....

3 Key phrases

A Choose a subject line for each email. One of the subject lines in the box is not used.

> Action re contract   Meeting 14/5   Re your advertisement
>
> Special Offer!   Shipping confirmation   Regarding your order

Email 1

Subject: ....

Re your last email, we are in the process of arranging the meeting scheduled for 14 May, but there are still a few details I need from you. Do you want me to book hotel accommodation for you – or will you sort it out at your end? Also, can you send us something about the Barcelona project you were involved in last year? It would be helpful to have something to circulate before the meeting. Please send a copy of any relevant reports. Regards, Monica.

Email 2

Subject: ....

Sorry for the delay in replying – I've been out of the country on business. Unfortunately, the items you ordered are not in stock, but we're expecting delivery by the end of the week. I'll get back to you as soon as they arrive. If you need any more information, please feel free to contact me.

Email 3

Subject: ....

Luisa, I've emailed Michelle and Roberto about the changes to the contract. Shall I have a word with Michelle to make sure she understands what's going on? You work with Roberto – can you talk to him? Thanks for your help – I appreciate it.

Email 4

Subject: ....

Good news! Subscribers to our email newsletter can take advantage of fantastic price savings in our January sale. I've attached a pdf file that gives full details, or alternatively just click on the link below. You can order over the web or by email – our customer service staff are standing by. Looking forward to hearing from you soon.

Email 5

Subject: ....

Just a short note to let you know that we received your order. We can confirm that the items were sent by mail today. To track your order, click on the link below. If there's anything else, just let us know. Best wishes, Pierre.

Note:
- Subject lines should be very short and very clear. They should tell the reader exactly what is coming in the body of the email.
- The word 'Re' appears in two of the subject lines. It is short for 'Regarding ...'.

B Complete the table by matching an <u>underlined</u> phrase in section A with a similar phrase below.

Previous contact

With reference to your email sent (date), …   1   *Re your last email*

Reason for email

We are writing to inform you that …   2

Good news

You will be pleased to hear that …   3

We are able to confirm that …   4

Bad news/Apologising

I apologise for…   5

We regret to inform you that …   6

Requests

I'd be grateful if you could …   7

I would appreciate it if you could …   8

Offering help

Would you like me to …?   9

If you wish, I would be happy to …   10

Promising action

I will contact you again.   11

Attachments

Please find attached …   12

Final comments

Thank you for your help.   13

Do not hesitate to contact us again   14

if you need any further information.

Closing

We are looking forward to …   15

Yours / Yours sincerely   16

• **In general, do you think the phrases on the left in section B are more *informal* or more *formal* than those on the right?**

4 Opening and closing

A **Match the email beginnings (1–8) with the endings (a–h).**

Beginnings ...	... Endings
1 I am writing with regard to your recent email. We regret to inform you that there are no double rooms available for the nights you require. ..*c*..	a) Anyway, thanks again for inviting me, and I'm really looking forward to it. Do you want me to bring anything?
2 Thanks so much for the wonderful present. It's exactly the book that I wanted – how did you know? I'm really looking forward to reading it.	b) You know you can count on me if you need any support. I'll call you at the weekend to see how things are.
3 Patricia, I've just read your email. I'm so sorry to hear about what happened.	c) Should you need any further information about room availability, we will be happy to assist you.
4 Sorry, I can't make it to your birthday party at Fishers restaurant, as I'm away on that day.	d) I look forward to receiving this information as soon as possible.
5 I am mailing this via the 'Contact Us' link on your website. I'd like to know a few more details about the anti-virus software that's listed on the site.	e) It really is great news, and I'm sure that it's only the beginning of our work in the French market.
6 I am writing with reference to our order number GH67. The goods arrived this morning, but you only sent 200 pieces instead of the 300 that we ordered.	f) Please deal with this matter urgently. I expect a reply from you by tomorrow morning at the latest.
7 Yes! Great! I'd love to come to the party.	g) Thanks again for the gift, and give my regards to your family.
8 I've just heard from Antonio about the Paris contract. It's fantastic news – you worked really hard on this and you deserve the success.	h) Anyway, sorry again that I can't come, but have a great time. I hope we can meet up soon. What about going to see that new Speilberg film?

B   Match the beginning and ending pairs in section A with the descriptions (1–8) below.

1   An email asking for information. Neutral style.   *5d*

2   An email giving information. Formal style.   ....

3   An email accepting an invitation. Informal style.   ....

4   An email refusing an invitation. Informal style.   ....

5   An email of congratulations. Neutral style.   ....

6   An email of complaint. Formal style.   ....

7   An email of thanks. Neutral style.   ....

8   An email of sympathy. Informal style.   ....

C   Read the following sentences. Decide whether they are beginnings or endings. Then decide whether they are neutral or informal.

1	The computer network will be shut down for maintenance at 5pm on Thursday.	(Beg)/End	(Neut)/Inf
2	Oh, yes – I'll be back late tonight. Can you do the shopping and buy something nice for dinner? Thx.	Beg/End	Neut/Inf
3	I look forward to receiving your advice on this matter.	Beg/End	Neut/Inf
4	What a surprise – how nice to hear from you!	Beg/End	Neut/Inf
5	Bye for now. See you soon.	Beg/End	Neut/Inf
6	I hope that everything is okay, but do not hesitate to contact me if you need any clarification.	Beg/End	Neut/Inf
7	Please find attached my report, as promised in Friday's meeting.	Beg/End	Neut/Inf
8	I'm so happy for you! Write again soon and tell me how it's going.	Beg/End	Neut/Inf
9	We are writing to advise you about some changes in our price list.	Beg/End	Neut/Inf
10	If you'd like any more details, just let me know. I'm away all next week but Andrea is dealing with this in my absence.	Beg/End	Neut/Inf
11	Just a quick note to say I really enjoyed last night.	Beg/End	Neut/Inf
12	Simon and I have been talking about your holiday plans for next August. It looks like we won't be able to join you. I'm really sorry.	Beg/End	Neut/Inf

D   Look back at the examples in section C. Find:

a)   two written to someone unknown or little known.   *3 / 9*

b)   four written to colleagues, perhaps sent to several people.   *1 / 5 / 6 / 7, 10*

c)   five written to a friend.   *4 / 5 / 8 / 11 / 12*

d)   one written to a very close family member.   *2*

5 Giving news

A Decide whether the following would be used in a formal or informal email.

1 Further to our phone call, I now have the information you requested.   formal / informal

2 Thanks for your email – it was great to hear from you again.   formal / informal

3 I'm sorry I haven't written for ages, but I've been really busy.   formal / informal

4 With reference to your last email, I am writing to let you know …   formal / informal

B Rewrite the sentences below with the correct word order, beginning as shown.

1 I'm writing our appointment 6 June on Tuesday to confirm.
   I'm ....

2 Unfortunately, I will make the meeting not be able to on 6 June Tuesday.
   Unfortunately, ...

3 You has been accepted your application will be pleased to hear that.
   You ....

4 We inform you regret to that your application has been not successful.
   We ....

5 Bad afraid news I'm about next weekend our trip.
   Bad ....

6 You'll guess never happened what's!
   You'll ....

7 Here's the project on an update.
   Here's ....

C Look back at the sentences in section B. Find:

a) two written by a friend to another friend.   5 / 6

b) two written by a business person to a colleague, about a meeting.   ...... / ......

c) two written by a Human Resources manager to a candidate for a job.   ...... / ......

d) one written by a business person to a colleague, introducing general information.   ......

D Complete the emails by writing *one* word in each gap. Several answers may be possible.

> (1) ....*Further*.... to our phone call earlier today, I'm writing to (2) .... that I will be able to (3) .... the meeting next Monday as discussed. Looking (4) .... to seeing you then.

> With (5) .... to your last email, I am writing to (6) .... you know what's happening with the project. (7) ...., things are running a bit late. You can get the whole picture from my report, which I've (8) .... as a Word doc.

E Match the verb forms in *italics* (a–f) with their uses (1–6) below.

a) Hi Anna. I'm in Switzerland! I'm *working* as an au-pair over the summer. ✓

b) I've got a new job! The hours *aren't* too bad – I *start* at 9 and *finish* around 5. ✓

c) I've got a new job! I've *been* so busy that I *haven't had* a chance to write. 6

d) You won't believe it! I *was shopping* in the city centre the other day and I saw Helga!

e) You won't believe it! I was shopping in the city centre the other day and I *saw* Helga! 3

f) Do you fancy going out on Friday? I've *been writing* a report all week and I need a break.

1   a habit or routine .b..
2   a temporary action in progress at the moment .a..
3   an action in progress in the past (gives the background) .d..
4   a completed action (we know when it happened) .e..
5   giving recent news (the writer's attention is on the present result of the events) .c..
6   an action in progress from the past up to the present .f..

F Read the email. Then choose the best word to fill each gap from A, B, C or D below.

Hi Angela, thanks for your email. I (1) *D* from you for ages! Was it really a year (2) *B* that we (3) *C* at the English Centre? Do you know, I've (4) *C* forgotten the name of our teacher! Anyway, I'm pleased to hear that you're (5) *B* enjoying your job, and that your relationship with Carlos (6) *A* well.
Yes, I know it's been ages (7) *D* I last emailed you too, but I've been really busy. (8) *A* the last few months (9) *D* at a wine bar. I start work at six every evening, and (10) *A* until midnight. I'm trying to save some money to go to Thailand, but I haven't got enough (11) *C* . I'm really enjoying it now, although at first it (12) *C* difficult. There are always so many people ordering things at the same time.
By the way, I (13) *D* to Manuella on the phone the other day and she (14) *B* you might come over here for a visit. Please do – you know you're always welcome to stay at our house.

	A	B	C	D
1)	A have heard	B don't hear	C did hear	D haven't heard ✓
2)	A before	B ago ✓	C previous	D since ✓
3)	A have been	B did be	C were	D are
4)	A still ✓	B yet	C already ✓	D however
5)	A yet	B still ✓	C longer	D soon
6)	A is going	B goes	C went	D go
7)	A for	B already	C while	D since
8)	A For ✓	B As	C While	D Since
9)	A I work ✓	B I had worked	C I worked	D I've been working ✓
10)	A I don't leave	B I'm not leaving	C I haven't left	D I'm not going to leave
11)	A already	B still	C yet ✓	D soon
12)	A has been	B had been	C was ✓	D is
13)	A talk	B have talked	C have been talking ✓	D was talking ✓
14)	A mentions	B mentioned ✓	C has mentioned	D has been mentioning

6 Information, action, help

A Complete the emails below by writing *one* word in each gap. Several answers may be possible.

> I've just (1)................................ your advertisement in Business Weekly for the seminar in Toulouse on
> 'The Internet As A Marketing Tool'. (2)................................ send me details. Also, (3)................................ you
> send me a list of hotels in Toulouse? Thank you for your (4)................................ , and I look forward to
> (5)................................ from you soon.
> (6)................................ , Naomi Chandler.

> Thank you for your email received today (7)................................ our seminar in Toulouse. You will find full
> details in the (8)................................ pdf document. Alternatively, you can visit our website at
> www.euroconference.com where you can also make an on-line booking.
> If you (9)................................ more information, please don't (10)................................ to contact me.

B Match the beginnings of the sentences (1–10) with the endings (a–j).

	1	Please get back to me if _b_	a)	your help on this
Information	2	I'd like to know a _c_	b)	you need any more information
	3	I'd appreciate _a_	c)	little more about
	4	I'll _f_	d)	there at the meeting
Action	5	I need you to be _d_	e)	you to prepare a report
	6	I'd like _e_	f)	send it to you
	7	Let me know if _h_	g)	I show them round
	8	Of course, I'd be _j_	h)	there's anything else
Help	9	Can I ask you to look _i_	i)	after them
	10	Shall _g_	j)	pleased to help

C Put the complete phrases from section B into the three emails below. The emails all include replies beginning with the symbol '>'.

Information

> Helen – I believe that you have had contact with EDF in the past. I'm going to their offices next Tuesday and
> (1).. them. In particular, can you tell me something about
> Henri Roland, their sales director? Have you met him? (2).. .
> Thanks, Martin.
> > EDF are quite a big operation – I've attached a Word doc with some background stuff. I've met Henri several
> times and I think he's someone we can work with. (3)..
> .... Helen

Action

> Bob – the management committee are meeting on 14 Feb and they're going to discuss last year's figures. ⁽⁴⁾_____ for the meeting. Could you do it by the end of next week? I know it's short notice. And ⁽⁵⁾_____ in case there's any questions I can't answer. Thanks, Lara.
>
> > I'll start the report right away, and ⁽⁶⁾_____ in a day or two. I've made a note of the meeting in my diary and I'll be there.

Help

> Alan – I know you're very busy at the moment, but I need some help. I have a group of visitors from Hungary coming on Wednesday afternoon after lunch. Unfortunately, I can't be back in the office until about 3pm. ⁽⁷⁾_____ until I get back? I'd really appreciate it. Thanks, Isabella.
>
> > ⁽⁸⁾_____ . ⁽⁹⁾_____ the building and introduce them to Roger and Sue? ⁽¹⁰⁾_____ I can do.

D Find the informal/neutral phrases from the three emails in section C that mean the same as the more formal phrases below. Write your answers.

Information

Could you give me some information about …   1 *I'd like to know a little more about*

If I can be of any further assistance, please do   2 ....
not hesitate to contact me.   ....

Thank you in advance for your help in this matter.   3 ....

Action

It is very important for me that you …   4 ....

Do you think you could …?   5 ....

Help

Would you like me to …?   6 ....

I would be very grateful for your help.   7 ....

Would you mind … (+ *-ing*)   8 ....

Please contact me again if …   9 ....

Certainly.   10 ....

7 Internal messages

A   **Read these two emails. Which one is better? Why?**

Version 1

> Subject: Visit of Mr Bianchi from Ferrara Textiles to our company tomorrow
>
> Tomorrow we will have the pleasure to welcome Mr Bianchi from Ferrara Textiles as a visitor to our company. His company intends to place a large order with us, and we hope that this will become a long-term business relationship. It is therefore very important to make a good impression, and all the staff in your department should know about his visit and be as helpful as possible. They should greet him by name, answer any questions he asks, explain procedures etc. He will be looking around the company from about 12.00, after his meeting with me. I would like to make sure that there is someone present in every section over the lunch period, in case he has any questions. Thank you for your cooperation in this matter.

Version 2

> Subject: Visit tomorrow
>
> Mr Bianchi of Ferrara Textiles will be looking around the company tomorrow, from about 12.00. It is important to make a good impression. Please:
> 1 Inform all staff in your department.
> 2 Remind them to greet Mr Bianchi by name and take time to answer his questions.
> 3 Arrange lunch breaks so that there is always someone available in your section.
> Thank you for your cooperation.

Compare your answer with the answer at the back of the book.

Note the following points about internal notes and messages:

- Separate points are used to refer to information or action.
- The points can be organised by numbers, or headings, or bullet points (like this).
- The style is clear and direct; sentences are short and have a simple structure.
- The language is neutral, not informal.
- If the memo refers to action, imperative verb forms are common (*Inform ...*, *Prepare ...*).
- Useful endings: *Thank you for your cooperation.* / *Please contact me if there are any problems.*

B   **First read the information below. Then identify the four stages in email version 2, section A.**

A typical structure for *any* piece of written communication, short message or longer report, is:

Situation ⇨ Problem or Objective ⇨ Solution or Strategy ⇨ Closing comment

C Rewrite the email. The maximum length is **80 words**, including the subject line. Think carefully about what information you need to include. <u>Underline</u> the key words to help you.

> Subject: Training course in how to use spreadsheets
> I have found some interesting information about a computer training course taking place in the city centre. I think it would be useful for someone from our department to attend as we are all a bit uncertain about how to use Excel, although we know the basics of course. I have a copy of their leaflet, and the details are as follows. The name of the course is 'Spreadsheets for Financial Planning', and the course dates are from 4 June to 8 June. The course runs every evening during that week, from 18.00 to 19.30. The cost is €750. I am free at that time and I would really like to go – I can help other people in the future. I know it's a bit expensive, but do you think the company can pay for me? I can't afford to pay for it out of my own money. Thank you very much.

Subject: ....

....

....

....

....

....

....

....

D Rewrite the email. The maximum length is **80 words**, including the subject line. Think carefully about what information you need to include. <u>Underline</u> the key words to help you.

> Subject: Mrs Rothe's retirement at the end of the year
> As you may know, Mrs Rothe will be retiring at the end of the year. She has made a great contribution to our company, and will be missed by all her colleagues. She has been with the company for fifteen years, moving up from Sales Assistant to Sales Manager during that time. To show our appreciation, we would like to organise a small leaving party for Mrs Rothe, after work on her final day. We will also present her with a small gift. I have asked Claudia to organise the collection for the gift, and she will be coming round with a large brown envelope if you want to make a contribution – the amount you give is entirely your choice. The leaving party will be after work on 20 December, in the main conference room. Everyone is welcome, and we hope that as many people as possible will come to say goodbye to Mrs Rothe. I look forward to seeing you there.

Subject: ....

....

....

....

....

....

8 Attachments

A In each gap there are *two* possible answers from A, B, C or D. Write both answers. The first one has been done for you.

1 Please _B/C_ my report. Hope it's useful.
    A find attachment   **C** find attached
    B find enclosed   **D** see attached

2 Here is my report. If there are any problems, _A/D_ me know.
    A please let   **C** please to let
    B make   **D** just let

3 This report has just arrived. I'm _B/D_ it to you. Hope it's not too late.
    A moving   **C** replying
    B forwarding   **D** sending

4 I'm sending various forms for you to complete. Please _B/D_ special attention to AF200.
    A give   **C** make
    B pay   **D** take

5 Please complete the attached forms, and return them to me _A/C_ 3 June.
    A by   **C** before
    B until   **D** to

6 As agreed, I'm sending the pre-meeting notes. Let me know if there's anything else we can do _B/C_ before we meet.
    A from our part   **C** on our side
    B from this end   **D** on this way

7 I'm attaching the Business Plan Review. Please _C/D_ that several alterations in dates have been made.
    A look   **C** note
    B appoint   **D** be aware

8 Please find attached my report. _C/B_ if there are any problems with deadlines etc.
    A Get back with me   **C** Get back to me
    B Get in touch   **D** Make a touch

9 Please find attached my report. _A/B_
    A Let me know what you think.   **C** Let me have what you think.
    B Let me have any comments.   **D** Make me have any comments.

10 Here is the itinerary for Sri Lanka. Please _A/D_ that I have included everything you want in it.
    A check   **C** control
    B agree   **D** confirm

B There is one mistake in each of these sentences. Correct it.

1 Here's the report – hope you like ^*it*.

2 Attached are the two questionnaires – please return them me by 24 September.

3 I sending the report as an attachment.

4 I'm sorry you couldn't open the document – I have attach it again.

5 Hope you'll be capable to open the document this time!

6 Please check the attached document careful and let me know if you have any questions.

7 I be grateful if you could complete the attached form and return it asap.

8 Sorry, I forgot send the attachment!

9 I attach my report like promised.

10 Here's a copy of Leslie's report – what you think?

11 Thanks for sending me the report – I let you know what I think.

12 I'm returning your original document with my comments inserted with red.

C Complete the emails by writing *one* word in each gap. There may be several possible answers.

Email 1

Please (1)................... attached my report. (2)................... it's not too late. (3)................... me know if you have any questions.

Email 2

I'm (1)................... various forms for you to complete. Please pay special (2)................... to the expenses claim form. I need them back (3)................... 16 February at the latest.

Email 3

(1)................... agreed, I'm sending the pre-meeting notes. Let me know if there's anything (2)................... we can do from this (3)................... before we meet.

Email 4

Sorry, I (1)................... to send the attachment! (2)................... it is. Please get (3)................... to me if you can't open it.

Email 5

I (1)................... be grateful if you (2)................... complete the attached form and return it asap. Please (3)................... that I have changed my email address.

9 Arranging a meeting

A **Look at the words and phrases in *italics*. In each case two are natural but *one* is not. Cross out the word or phrase that is *not* natural. The symbol '–' means no word.**

1   What time would *be convenient for/be convenient/suit* you?

2   Are you free *sometime/anytime/one time* next week?

3   Could we *meet on/–/at* Thursday *during/on/in* the afternoon? Perhaps *on/–/at* 3pm?

4   Yes, I think I *shall/should/would* be able to make next Friday morning.

5   I'll *email/return to/get back to* you later today to confirm it.

6   I'm out of the office *for/until/till* 2pm on that day. Anytime after that *could be/is/would be* fine.

7   I'm afraid I'm *busy/occupied/tied up* all day next Tuesday.

8   *Pardon me,/Sorry,/I'm afraid* I can't *make/control/manage* it on that day.

9   Sorry, I've already got *an arrangement/an appointment/a promise* on that day.

10   *What if/What about/How about* Wednesday *instead/in place of/as an alternative*?

11   Would you *mind/matter/object* if we put the meeting *back/off/away* to the following week?

12   I *am very sorry/regret again/apologise again* for any inconvenience caused.

13   I look forward to *see/seeing/speaking to* you next week.

14   Give me a *call/telephone/ring* if you have any problems.

15   Give my *regards/best wishes/compliments* to Herr Schrempp.

B **Complete the sequence of emails by writing *one* word in each gap. Several answers may be possible.**

> Günter – we need to meet to discuss the budget for next year. Could we meet (1)............................ Friday
> (2)............................ the morning? Let me know if that would be (3)............................ for you. I hope
> everyone in the Berlin office is well. Give my (4)............................ to Kristina and Alex.
> Bw, Susanna.

> Susanna, I'm (5)............................ I can't (6)............................ it next Friday – I'm (7)............................ all
> day. (8)............................ about Monday 12th (9)............................ ? I should be (10)............................ to
> make a morning meeting, otherwise anytime after 4pm (11)............................ be fine.
> Hope that's okay, Günter.

> Günter, yes – Monday morning is good for me too. Shall we say 9.30? I look forward to (12)............................
> you then. Give me a (13)............................ if you have (14)............................ problems.
> Susanna.

C   Match the beginnings and endings of the phrases below.

1 are we still okay _b_
2 can we reschedule for _e_
3 I'll circulate _d_
4 I need to _a_
5 let me know if you _f_
6 something urgent _c_

a) finalise arrangements today.
b) for Tuesday?
c) has come up.
d) the agenda in the next few days.
e) the following week?
f) want to make any changes.

D   Put the complete phrases from section C into the three emails below.

Charles-Henri, (1) ....? Please get back to me this morning if possible as (2) ....
Natalia.

Natalia, I'm sorry to ask this at such short notice, but (3) ....
........................? Perhaps Wednesday 24th? I do apologise, but (4) ....
.... I hope it won't inconvenience you too much.
Charles-Henri.

Okay, let's make it Wednesday 24th. (5) ....
Please (6) ....
Natalia.

E   First, review some grammar for planning a trip, then complete the email from a secretary by putting the verbs in brackets into a form of *will* or the present continuous.

The *will* form (*I'll do* …) and the present continuous (*I'm doing* …) can both be used for talking about the future, but there is a small difference:

- *will* is used for facts and general beliefs.
- present continuous is used for arrangements (with a time and a place).

As you know, you (1) _'re going_ (go) to Brussels on Wednesday. I've spoken to Mr Cuvier's secretary and the details of the trip are now more or less planned. You (2) .... (catch) the 8.00 flight from City Airport. Someone (3) .... (be) at the airport to take you to the hotel – you (4) .... (stay) at the Marriot for just one night. At 11.00 you (5) .... (meet) Mr Cuvier at his office. I'm sure he (6) .... (take) you out to lunch. After lunch you (7) .... (not/do) anything until 4pm, so you (8) .... (have) time to go back to the hotel if you want. The travel agency (9) .... (send) the tickets here by courier this afternoon, so I (10) .... (give) them to you as soon as they arrive.

10 Invitations and directions

A Look at the phrases in *italics* in the three emails below. One phrase in each pair comes from a company with a formal culture, the other phrase comes from a company with an informal culture. <u>Underline</u> all the phrases from the formal company.

Email 1

(1)*Dear Mary*/Hi Mary
(2)*I'm writing to invite you/We would be very pleased if you could come* to a meeting here on 14 May. (3)*It has been arranged/I've arranged it* to bring together all our colleagues working in Central Europe (4)*to/in order to* share experiences about working in this market. (5)*Your attendance will be very welcome/It'd be great to see you.*
The meeting will last all day and will have an informal agenda – (6)*you won't need to/it will not be necessary to* write a report for it or make a presentation. (7)*Refreshments will be provided/There'll be plenty to eat and drink* during the day.
(8)*Hope to see you in May!/Your presence at the meeting will be very useful.* Please let me know if you (9)*will be able to attend/can make it,* (10)*asap/as soon as possible.*
Best regards, (11)*John Saunders/Stephanie*

Email 2

(12)*Thanks a lot for the invite/Thank you for your kind invitation.* (13)*I would be delighted to attend/I'd love to come to* the meeting. (14)*It sounds like a great idea/I am sure it will be very useful.* Please let me know if there's anything I can do to help from this end.
(15)*Will it be okay/Would it be possible* to bring Martina Rutka as well? She's a new member of our team and is very involved with the Central Europe market. (16)*Thanks again/Thank you once more for your invitation,* and (17)*I look forward to seeing you/see you* on 14 May.

Email 3

(18)*Thanks a lot for the invite/Thank you for your kind invitation.* Unfortunately, I have another appointment on that day. (19)*I'm very sorry that I will miss the meeting/Please accept my apologies.*
In any case, send my regards to everyone at the meeting, and please (20)*let me have a copy of any report arising from the discussion/email me and let me know how it went.*
I hope (21)*we can meet up soon/we will have the opportunity to meet on another occasion in the near future.*
(22)*Good luck with the meeting!/I am sure that the meeting will be a great success.*

Basics

B Complete the phrases by writing *one* word in each gap. Several answers may be possible.

1 We .... be very pleased if you .... come to a meeting here on 28 July.

2 Your .... at the meeting will be very .... I hope you can .... it.

3 Please .... me .... if you can attend, ... soon as possible.

4 Thank you for your .... invitation. I would be .... to attend. I look forward to .... you on the 28th.

5 .... , I will not be able to come. I have another .... on that day. Please accept my ....

6 I hope we will have the .... to meet on another occasion in the .... future. I am sure the meeting will be a great ....

C Put these sentences into the correct order.

a) Looking forward to meeting you next week.

b) Our office is located close to the station – the best thing to do is catch a taxi.

c) Just to confirm your visit to us on 16 Jan.

d) Best wishes, Atsuko.

e) When you arrive, ask for me at reception and I will come down and meet you.

f) If you need to contact me, my mobile number is 07968 243983.

   1 .... 2 .... 3 .... 4 .... 5 .... 6 ....

D Review some language for giving directions and planning an informal visit. Complete the email below by writing *one* word in each gap.

Here are the directions for how to (1)........................ to my house – print out this email and bring it with you. It's not difficult to (2)........................ , as you're coming (3)........................ train. Come out of the station and (4)........................ right. Carry (5)........................ down the road (6)........................ you come to a church called St Paul's. You can't (7)........................ it. Just after the church turn left. Be careful – it's a very small street and people often go (8)........................ without noticing it. You'll see my house (9)........................ the end of the street – it's got a red door. Try and get here (10)........................ time for lunch. You can (11)........................ me a call on your mobile if you get (12)........................ .

After lunch there's a couple of things we could (13)........................ . (14)........................ we can look around Brighton, or we can take my car and go for a walk in the (15)........................ . We don't need to decide (16)........................ – we'll just see how we're (17)........................ at the time. It's great that you're coming down to (18)........................ for a few days. I'm really (19)........................ forward to it. Give my best (20)........................ to your family.

11 Negotiating a project

A <u>Underline</u> the correct word.

1 *Can*/*Shall* you give me some information about …?

2 I *will*/*would* be grateful if you *should*/*could* give me some information about …

3 Do you think you *would*/*could* send me more details?

4 We *necessary to*/*need to* discuss this before we go any further.

5 How do you think we *should*/*shall* deal with this?

6 I *will*/*would* appreciate your advice.

7 We *would*/*should* be prepared to give you a discount if you …

8 That *can*/*could* be possible.

9 That *shall*/*should* be possible.

10 That *might*/*would* be possible – I need to ask my line manager.

11 No problem – that *might*/*would* be possible.

12 I think we *must to have*/*need to have* a meeting to discuss this in more detail.

13 Let me know what time *should*/*would* suit you best.

14 I'm sorry that we *couldn't*/*wouldn't* use your services this time.

B Put the phrases (a–j) with their correct headings below.

a) Let's talk next week and see how things are going.	f) Would you be able to …?
b) I can see what you're saying, but …	g) I am willing to … (if …)
c) Can you give me some more information about …?	h) What about if we …?
d) What do you think is the best way forward?	i) The main thing for me is …
e) I'm sorry that we couldn't use your services this time, but I hope there will be another opportunity.	j) That's fine.

1 **Asking for information**   What are your usual charges (fees/rates) for …? *C*

2 **Requests**   Do you think you could …? ....

3 **Emphasising a main point**   My main concern at this stage is … ....

4 **Asking for a suggestion**   How do you think we should deal with this? ....

5 **Making a suggestion**   Why don't you …? ....

6 **Negotiating: being firm**   I understand what you're saying about …, but … ....

7 **Negotiating: being flexible**   We would be prepared to … (if …) ....

8 **Negotiating: agreeing**   Okay, I'm happy with that for now. ....

9 **Next steps**   I'll be in touch again soon with more details. ....

10 **Closing**   I look forward to working with you. ....

C Complete the sequence of emails by using the phrases (1–10) in section B.
NB: Not the phrases in the box.

Dear Ms Dupuis
Your name was given to me by Dominique Clement at Toulouse Business Services. I understand that you recently did some IT training for them on a freelance basis. We need some training along similar lines for our staff, and I am in the process of looking at different options. I would be grateful if you could give me the following information:
(1) .... this kind of work?
Are you available in early September?
Also, some of our older software needs upgrading or replacing before we have the training, and the original supplier has gone out of business. (2) .... ?
I would appreciate your advice.
I look forward to hearing from you soon.
Regards, Karl Finlay

Dear Karl, thank you for your email. I attach a pdf file with our current rates and a list of recent clients. Early September looks fine at the moment – can you let me know the dates, times, number of participants etc?
In relation to your final point, (3) .... send someone to the Software and Services Exhibition in Lyon next month? A lot of suppliers have stands there.
Best wishes, Cristine

Cristine, Thanks for the quick reply.
(4) .... the cost, and we need to discuss this before we go any further. I need to know that we will get good value for money.
(5) .... send me more details of your course programme and your training methods?
You wanted some more information from us. I'm afraid I don't have the exact dates etc. at the moment, but (6) ....

Karl, I attach a typical course programme for you to have a look at, although at this stage it's difficult to be too specific about your particular course.
(7) .... give you a discount of 10% on the prices I quoted earlier, if you paid half the total amount in advance.
(8) .... value for money, but our training programmes are competitively priced and I can assure you that we have always had very good feedback.

Cristine, (9) .... I think we need to have a meeting to discuss the training course in more detail. I'm free most mornings – let me know when would suit you best. In the meantime, I'm attaching a document that lists all the hardware we currently have in the office, and the new software we are going to install. Let me know if you need any more information before the meeting.
(10) .... Karl

12 Checking understanding

A Read the email exchange between Peter and Kate. In each gap there are *two* missing words – try to guess what they are. In email 2 Kate has used the 'Reply' button, so she includes the text of the email she received.

Email 1 (from Peter to Kate)

> Kate, I've attached the sales figures for Q3, as requested.
> You'll see that we're up 6%! Things are really taking off in Central Europe.
> By the way, are you going to the conference?

Email 2 (from Kate to Peter)

> > Kate, I've attached the sales figures for Q3, as requested.
> Sorry, Peter, you forgot to send (1)_____ _____ . Can you send it again?
> > You'll see that we're up 6%! Things are really taking off in Central Europe.
> Great news. Do (2)_____ _____ 6% increase for the quarter or for the whole year?
> > By the way, are you going to the conference?
> (3)_____ _____ ? The sales conference in Istanbul next month or the International
> Plastics Convention in Slough?

Email 3 (from Peter to Kate)

> Sorry about that, Kate. Here it is again. Let (4)_____ _____ if you get it.
> I meant 6% for the quarter! Head Office are very pleased.
> What do you mean 'Which conference?'!! I was talking about the sales conference of course. But are
> (5)_____ _____ it's in Istanbul?

Email 4 (from Kate to Peter)

> Okay, I've got the attachment this time. But you'll never believe it – I can't (6)_____
> _____ ! Can you check that you've saved it properly?
> I thought the conference was in Istanbul, but I may (7)_____ _____ . I'll check and
> get back (8)_____ _____ . Anyway, I can't go this year – Cathy is going instead.

Before you look at the answers in the back of the book, here are all the words you need:

attachment	be	conference	it	know	me	mean	open	sure	to
the	which	wrong	you	you	you				

B Fill in the missing prepositions. Each gap represents one word.

1 To copy somebody _____ an email.   (= to send somebody a copy of an email)
2 To get _____ somebody about something.   (= to contact somebody again)

C Rewrite the sentences below with the correct word order to make typical email phrases. Start each sentence with a capital letter.

1 sorry, you forgot the send to attachment. you can again send it?

....

2 mean you to send this did? i don't want the attachment to open in case it's a virus got.

....

3 about that are you sure? i thought was in Istanbul the conference.

....

4 i'll check and get you back to later today.

....

5 you do mean which conference?

....

6 i don't this point understand sorry. can you in a little detail more explain it?

....

7 i'm sure not what mean you by this. you could clarify?

....

8 i thought on Thursday was the meeting, but I wrong may be.

....

9 sorry, my last email forget. you're right. not Friday, it should Thursday be.

....

10 what was meant I Gatwick, not Heathrow. the situation this clarifies i hope.

....

D The email below shows some original text introduced with a '>' symbol, and some comments in *italics*. Complete the email by writing *one* word in each gap.

> I've written down some thoughts about the Beta project – it's (1)........................ as a Word doc. I'm circulating it to all line managers. (2)........................ me know what you think.
I'm afraid you (3)........................ to send the attachment. Can you send it (4)........................ ?
> There's a couple of things I'd like you focus on. First is the timing.
I'm not sure what you mean (5)........................ 'timing'. The time before the project starts, or the time the project will actually take once it's started?
> Then there's the question of marketing costs.
I know Daniel produced some detailed figures on this some time ago. Have you (6)........................ with him?
> Finally, feasibility.
I don't understand this (7)........................ . Can you explain in a little more (8)........................ ?
> I'd like your comments by the end of next week at the (9)........................ .
Okay, I'll try to get them (10)........................ to you by then.
One last thing – I think you need to copy Lila (11)........................ on your original email. I may be (12)........................ , but I think she's now involved from the Latin America end.

13 Verb forms

A Match a *form* in the left-hand column with a *meaning* in the middle column and a *grammar word* in the right-hand column.

1 Sales *increase* every year.	a) Completed actions in a completed period of time.	past simple
2 Sales *are increasing* at the moment.	b) Actions and situations repeated regularly over a long period of time.	past continuous
3 Sales *have increased* by 5% this year.	c) Actions or situations in progress from the past up to the present.	present simple
4 Sales *have been increasing* rapidly this year.	d) Temporary actions and situations in progress now.	present continuous
5 Sales *increased* significantly last year.	e) Actions or activities in progress in the past.	present perfect
6 Sales *were increasing* all through last year.	f) A past event or situation that is connected to the present.	present perfect continuous

Note: remember that some verbs are not normally used in a continuous form. These include verbs of thinking (*doubt, know, understand*), the senses (*see, appear*), feelings (*like, want, hope*), possession (*belong to, contain, have*) and other verbs like *cost, depend on, mean, need*.

B Write the time phrases from the box below in the column where they are used most often. Some of the phrases can be used in more than one column.

ago   already   always/often/never   at the moment   currently   ever   every day from time to time   in the nineties   just   last week   not yet   now   nowadays   once a year over the last few months   recently   so far this year   these days   up to now   yesterday

Present simple *(I do)*	Present continuous *(I am doing)*	Present perfect *(I have done)*	Past simple *(I did)*

Note: time phrases help to make the meaning clear and are usually associated with particular verb forms.

C Complete the email by putting the verb in brackets into either the present simple (*I do*), present continuous (*I'm doing*) or present perfect (*I've done*). The time phrases will help you. Use contractions where appropriate.

Every year around this time we (1).......................... (interview) candidates for functions across the company. This week I (2).......................... (plan) that process, so I (3).......................... (need) an estimate of staffing needs from every department. In past years we (4).......................... (always/be able to) recruit the numbers asked for, but this year will be different. At the moment we (5).......................... (operate) in a difficult market, and sales (6).......................... (fall) considerably over the last year. This (7).......................... (mean) that we will have to reduce our staffing costs, although I (8).......................... (hope) it will only be temporary.

D Complete the email by putting the verb in brackets into either the present simple (*I do*), present perfect (*I've done*) or past simple (*I did*). The time phrases will help you. Use contractions where appropriate.

I (1).......................... (just/receive) an email from our subsidiary in Russia. They (2).......................... (need) more brochures as they (3).......................... (give out) their entire stock over the last few months. They (4).......................... (have) a stand at the Moscow Trade Fair last week and (5).......................... (distribute) hundreds of brochures. Now they (6).......................... (want) us to send another 5,000 copies. I (7).......................... (already/contact) Sales to see if they have any spare, but I (8).......................... (think) we'll need some more. Can you get a quotation from the printers?

E Complete the email by putting the verb in brackets into either the present perfect (*I've done*), past simple (*I did*) or past continuous (*I was doing*). The time phrases will help you. Use contractions where appropriate.

Hi Isabel! Sorry I (1).......................... (not/be) in touch recently. Hope you're well. Guess what! The other day I (2).......................... (meet) Katia while I (3).......................... (wait) at the bus stop. Remember her? That girl from Russia who (4).......................... (be) in our English class last year. I almost (5).......................... (not/recognise) her because she (6).......................... (wear) sunglasses and she (7).......................... (dye) her hair pink! Anyway, she said that she (8).......................... (go out) for a drink next Friday and she invited us. Do you want to come?

F Complete the email by putting the verb in brackets into the present perfect (*I've done*) or the present perfect continuous (*I've been doing*). Use contractions where appropriate.

Are you there? I (1).......................... (phone) all week and there's no answer! I couldn't email you because I (2).......................... (wait) to get my computer fixed. What's your news? (3).......................... (you/find) a job yet? As for me, I (4).......................... (decide) to get fit. Yes, really! I (5).......................... (diet), and I (6).......................... (start) yoga classes as well. I (7).......................... (go) for a couple of weeks now and I'm really enjoying it. (8).......................... (you/ever/do) yoga? Anyway, get in touch when you have a chance.

14 Comparisons

A **Complete the words with the missing letters.**

Comparatives and superlatives of adjectives

1	fast	fast**er**	the fast _est_ (one syllable adjectives)
2	big	big**ger**	the big_____ (ending in one short vowel + consonant)
3	easy	eas_____	the eas_____ (ending -y)
4	expensive	**more/l**_____ expensive	the **most/l**_____ expensive (two/three/four syllable adjectives)
5	good/bad	**better/w**_____	**the best/w**_____ (irregular adjectives)
6	far	**fur**_____	**the fur**_____ (irregular adjective)

Useful phrases

7 A is more expensive **t**_____ B.

8 A is **a lot/m**_____ **more** expensive than B.

9 A is **a bit/a li**_____ **more** expensive than B.

10 A is o_____ **of our b**_____ selling models.

11 A costs **20% m**_____ **t**_____ B.

12 It's colder and cold**er/m**_____ **and m**_____ difficult.

13 **The be**_____ the quality, **t**_____ **m**_____ you pay.

14 It was **the b**_____ meal I've e_____ **eaten.**

15 A is cheap **com**_____ **to/in com**_____ **with** B.

16 A is (almost/twice/not) _____ expensive _____ B.

17 A is (exactly/almost/nearly/not) **the s**_____ **a**_____ B.

18 I don't have **as m**_____ friends as in England.

19 I don't have **as m**_____ time as I used to.

20 Bill is (exactly/just/quite/not) **li**_____ his brother.

B <u>Underline</u> **the correct words or phrases in the email.**

Hi Yuko! I'm writing from an Internet café in the village of Dingle on the west coast of Ireland. I got a week's holiday from work so I came over here for a short break. I'm having a great time. It's so different compared (1)*for/to* England – even (2)*rainier/rainyer* if you can believe it!

I flew to Dublin first, and I spent a couple of days there – not as (3)*much/many* time as you really need because there's so much to see. The people are some of the (4)*friendliest/friendlier* I've (5)*never/ever* met.

I found the Irish accent quite difficult at first, but I'm getting (6)*more and more/always more* used to it. It's not cheap here – prices in Dublin were about the same (7)*than/as* London, but here on the coast they're (8)*more expensive/expensiver*.

I arrived here yesterday, and I can promise you, the west coast of Ireland is just (9)*as/so* beautiful as they say – it's so green. There's live music in the pubs at night, and the later it gets the (10)*more/most* people come in. That's all for now – I'm off to hear some music! Write soon. Justine.

C Complete the email by writing *one* word in each gap.

Thank you for your email inquiring about our products.

We have three optical pen scanners in our range, the 400C, 600C and 800C. A pen scanner is (1) __*like*__ a hand-held scanner, you scan in text from a page and download it into your PC or PDA later. The 800C is our (2) _____ selling model, and has (3) _____ widest range of functions, including a translating dictionary. The 600C is similar (4) _____ the 800C, but has (5) _____ memory – it can only store 1,000 pages of text, (6) _____ to 2,000 pages for the 800C. The 400C is cheaper (7) _____ the other two models, and doesn't have as (8) _____ memory or functionality. It's a more basic model, but its ability to scan text is just the (9) _____ . You will find full product and price details in the attached document.

In your email you ask about our terms of payment for large orders. Clearly, the bigger your order, the (10) _____ discount we can give. Our normal minimum order is 500 units, but for a first-time customer we would accept an order (11) _____ small as 200 units. It would be better to discuss all this in more detail at a later date, but I'm sure you'll find our terms are very competitive in comparison (12) _____ other suppliers. We're confident that these pens will sell very well in your market, and customer feedback on the 800C is amongst the best we have (13) _____ had.

If you have any (14) _____ questions, please do not hesitate to contact me.

D When we write or speak it can sound strange to give a very exact figure. Instead we use vague language. Complete the table with the phrases from the box.

a little over 50%   almost 50%   ~~a lot more than 50%~~   around 50%   far less than 50% considerably more than 50%   much less than 50%   nearly 50%   slightly more than 50% roughly 50%

70%	1a) _a lot more than 50%_		1b) _____	
54%	2a) _____		2b) _____	
48–52%	3a) _____		3b) _____	
46%	4a) _____		4b) _____	
30%	5a) _____		5b) _____	

E Complete the words in each sentence with the missing letters.

1 This year's sales were €5.5m – that's a li__ttle__ o__ver__ last year's figure of €5.2m.

2 This year's sales were €3.9m – that's mu_____ l_____ th_____ last year's figure of €5.2m.

3 This year's sales were €7.9m – that's a_____ d 50% up on last year's figure.

4 This year's sales were €7.6m – that's n_____ y 50% up on last year's figure.

5 This year's sales were €5.5m – that's sl_____ m_____ t_____ last year's figure of €5.2m.

6 This year's sales were €5.1m – that's r_____ the same _____ last year's figure.

15 Sentence structure

A **Read the information about sentence structure.**

A simple affirmative sentence in English typically has the order Subject + Verb + Object. Each part can be a phrase rather than a single word:

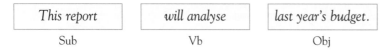

This report	will analyse	last year's budget.
Sub	Vb	Obj

There can be an adverb phrase as well, and it often comes at the end. Adverbs say how (*quickly*), where (*at our offices*) or when (*next week*) something happens. If we have several adverbs together, the usual word order is HOW – WHERE – WHEN. Look at these examples:

I	am looking forward	to our meeting	in Munich	next month.
Sub	Vb	Obj	Adv (where)	Adv (when)

Sales	rose	by over 10%	in Hungary	last year.	('rise' does not take an object)
Sub	Vb	Adv (how)	Adv (where)	Adv (when)	

Now rewrite the sentences (1–4) below with the correct word order. Start sentences with a capital letter.

1 me   you may   remember. we   business cards   last week   at the Trade Fair   exchanged.

....

2 well   is going   our advertising campaign. we should   until June   consider   extending it.

....

3 about availability of rooms   in July   to ask   I am writing. I need   for 3 nights   a single room.

....

4 next weekend   to my parents   I am going. for a long time   I haven't   them   seen.

....

B **Read the information on making complex sentences.**

You can make complex sentences by combining simple ones:

I	am sorry to say	I can't accept your invitation on this occasion	but	I
Sub	Vb	Obj		Sub

hope to make	another trip to Paris	when I have more time later this year.
Vb	Obj	Adv (when)

- There are two main clauses, joined by the linking word 'but'.
- The phrase *I can't … occasion* is a full clause, with a subject, verb, object and adverb.
- The phrase *I have … year* is a full clause, with a subject, verb, object and adverb.

Language focus

Now rewrite sentences (1–5) with the correct word order.

1 I am writing   to let you know   from Head Office in Munich   I am coming to visit   next month   that   your offices in Moscow.

....

....

2 This will be   in Central Europe   part of a visit   to all our subsidiaries   that   I am making.

....

....

3 to consult with you   I will take the opportunity   about our strategic plan   for Central Europe,   which   for some time   we have been working on.

....

....

4 I would also like   our production facility   while I am in Moscow   to visit   and if there is time,   as well   some of the local suppliers.

....

....

5 I will contact you again   when   I can travel   the exact dates   as soon as I know.

....

....

C **Put the lines in the emails below into the correct order.**

Email 1

I am writing to thank you *1*

The meetings were very productive, and *4*

As well as the business side of things, *7*

The next time that you are in Munich *11*

Please give my regards ......

for your hospitality ......

during my recent trip to Paris. ......

I really appreciated the time you took ......

I am sure that they lay the basis for ......

to show me Notre Dame, and ......

to your colleagues in the Paris office, ...

the wonderful meal that we had afterwards. ......

a good long-term business relationship. ......

it will be my pleasure to return your kindness. ......

it was a great pleasure to meet them all. *15*

Email 2

Thank you for taking the time to attend *1*

Unfortunately, we have to inform you that ......

As we mentioned in the interview, we had *5*

While we were impressed with your interview, *8*

We appreciate your interest in *12*

many applicants for this position ......

your application has not been successful. ......

an interview with us last week. ......

we did not feel ......

working with us, ...

that you have the necessary skills ......

and we would like to take this opportunity ......

and experience for the position. ......

and the standard of candidates was very high. ......

to wish you every success in the future. *15*

16 Common mistakes

A   Correct the mistake in each sentence.

1   ~~I am write~~ with regard to your recent email.   *I am writing*

2   Please send me your comments until Friday at the latest. ....

3   I will be grateful if you could send me more information. ....

4   Please find attach my report, as promised in Friday's meeting. ....

5   I hope we can to meet up soon. ....

6   I look forward to receiving this information so soon as possible. ....

7   I'm sorry I haven't written for ages, but I been really busy. ....

8   It will be more better for me if we meet on Tuesday rather than Monday. ....

9   Can we meet at 8 Feb at 14.30 instead? ....

10   Sorry, I don't can help you on this matter. ....

11   If you require any further informations, please do not hesitate to contact me. ....

12   I look forward to meet you next week. ....

13   I am really appreciate your kindness during my stay in London. ....

14   At the meeting we will discuss the follow points. ....

15   I'm afraid but we haven't received your payment yet. ....

B   Each phrase below has *one* word missing. Add the missing word.

1   With reference ^*to* your email sent 6 June, ...

2   Thank you sending me the catalogue I requested.

3   We are writing to inform that ...

4   We are able confirm that ...

5   I apologise the delay.

6   I would appreciate if you could ...

7   Please get back me if there's anything else.

8   What time would convenient for you?

9   If you like any more details, just let me know.

10   Anyway, that's enough, I think I stop writing now.

11   It was good to meet you the conference in Paris.

12   I look forward to hearing you soon.

13   I've attached a copy the latest sales figures.

14   Thank you for the invitation visit your company.

15   With reference your enquiry, I've attached all the information you need.

C Each *paragraph* in the emails below has *three* mistakes. Correct the mistakes.

Email 1

It was a pleasure to meet you in Budapest last week and I would like to thank you for your interest in our office products. You mentioned that you were going/visit Turkey soon, and when you do I like to invite you to visit our factory outside Istanbul. We would be very pleased to showing you round our new factory and modern production facilities.

As you would being our guest, we would of course arrange for you to stay in a good hotel and take you out to dinner. Please to let me know when you have finalised your travel plans. I look forward to see you in Turkey in the near future.

Email 2

You will all be aware that we been interviewing candidates for the position of Marketing Director. I am now pleased to inform that we have appointed an excellent candidate, Simone Verhart. Simone has worked in marketing for over fifteen years and I am sure that she will be a valuable member of team.

I would like to invite you a short lunchtime reception in Conference Room 2 next Tuesday 5 Feb where you will have chance to meet Simone on an informal basis. Refreshments will be available. Please let me know if you can come so that I can to estimate numbers.

Email 3

I am write re our order for 1,000 pieces of footwear, reference VK899. The money was transfer to your account on 23 January and we yet haven't received the goods. You promised in your email of 15 Dec that you would ship within 7 days of a firm order.

I called your office this morning but the secretary told that you were away until tomorrow (Thursday). Please call me at the morning and let me know what is happening. We have customers waiting for these pieces and the delay is causing us for to lose business.

Email 4

It has been brought to my attention that security in the building is not so good as it could be. As you may be aware, one of our secretaries had her bag stolen yesterday. In the light of this, I would like to remember you to take care of your personal possessions, particular at those times of the day when the building is not busy.

I am going to prepare a report on how security could be improved, and I could be grateful for any suggestions that you have. Please email me with your ideas by the end of next week at the later. I also have a word with our security staff in reception to see if there are any procedures we can improve there.

17 Punctuation and spelling

A Review the rules for full stops, commas and capital letters. Then rewrite the email, putting in a) capital letters b) *four* full stops and c) *two* commas.

A full stop (.) is used at the end of a sentence.

A comma (,) is used:

- like a brief pause in speech, to make the sentence easier to read.
- to separate words in a list (except for the last two items where we use *and*).
- after many linking words that come at the beginning of a sentence (like *However*).

Capital letters (also called 'upper case' letters) are used:

- to begin a sentence.
- for names of people, places, events and organisations.
- for job titles.
- for nationalities and languages.
- for calendar information like days, months etc.

> dear antoine curiel
>
> i am the sales manager for genetech a small biotechnology company based in cologne i attended your presentation at the eurotech conference in paris in november and we met briefly afterwards here is the information i said i would send including our latest annual report i hope it is of interest
>
> best regards
>
> michael bretz

....

....

....

....

....

....

B Review the rules for apostrophes. Then rewrite the email, putting in a) capital letters, b) apostrophes and c) *four* commas.

An apostrophe (') is used:

- in short forms to show that one or more letters have been left out
- before the possessive *-s* to show ownership or the relationship between people

> hi jean – how are you? thanks for your email about mr williams. in fact im meeting him on friday 16 march. were meeting in his brussels office and im a bit nervous about it because i dont speak french very well! hes the marketing director of the company and reports directly to the ceo. its going to be an interesting meeting and i havent been to belgium before so im looking forward to it. anyway ill be in touch when i get back.

....
....
....
....
....
....

C Review the rules for colons and semi-colons. Then rewrite the email, putting in a) capital letters, b) apostrophes, c) *two* commas, d) *one* colon and e) *two* semi-colons.

A colon (:) is used to introduce items in a list.
A semi-colon (;) is used to separate long items in a list, particularly if there are commas inside some items. It is also used to join two sentences with a related meaning (this is rare).

> Angela – have you read johns report yet? i think its main conclusions are correct. this is basically what hes saying sales are flat and have been so for months theres no new products in the pipeline despite our large r&d budget and our share price is at its lowest point since last november. i hope the board take it seriously.

....
....
....
....
....

D How good is your spelling? If you have a spell-checker that works with email then it is not really a problem, but many people don't. <u>Underline</u> the spelling mistakes in the email and write the correction below. There are 30 incorrect words.

> Hi Tim! Thanks for your email <u>wich</u> I recieved some time ago. Sorry I havn't replyed before now, but I've been realy busy. Actualy, it's good news – I've got a job! I went for loads of interviews and finaly I was sucessful – I'm working for a small indipendent record company. The job is very intresting – I help to organise tours for the groups, make arangements for there accomodation in the cityes where they play, things like that. I've been doing it since the begining of Februry, and its grate – completly difrent to my old job working in a restarant! It's a good oportunity for me. Hopefuly, if the peopel in the company like me, I'll get more responsabilities and more mony. Then I coud even think about visitting you in Ingland! Anyway, keep in touch, and I look foward to seeing you soon.

1 *which*	7	13	19	25
2	8	14	20	26
3	9	15	21	27
4	10	16	22	28
5	11	17	23	29
6	12	18	24	30

18   A customer–supplier sequence

A   **Match the words (1–5) with the definitions (a–e).**

1   a complaint ....   a)   a request to send goods
2   an invoice ....   b)   a request for general information
3   a quotation ....   c)   a request for payment
4   an inquiry ....   d)   something you say or write when you are not satisfied
5   an order ....   e)   a document giving detailed information about the cost of something

Find:

6   three documents above sent by the customer to the supplier .... / .... / ....

7   two documents above sent by the supplier to the customer .... / ....

B   **Complete this typical customer-supplier sequence with the words from the box.**

a complaint   information   ~~an inquiry~~   an invoice (with the goods)
an order   the problem   a quotation   the quotation

The customer...   The supplier...

1   makes   *an inquiry*......................   2   sends   ....

3   requests   4   gives   ....

5   makes   6   sends   ....

7   makes   8   solves   ....

C   **Below you will see eight emails between a supplier of ornamental plants and a hotel manager. Put them into the correct order. Section B will help you.**

(a)   Thank you for your email received today. We supply and maintain large, ornamental plants for hotel lobbies and company reception areas. We have been in business for more than ten years and have some of the city's biggest hotels among our clients. Please see the attached document for more details of our products and prices. If you need any more information, please let me know.

(b)   I saw your advertisement in a recent copy of Hotel and Catering Monthly. I am interested in your Plant Solutions service for hotel lobbies. Please send more details.

(c)   Your visit to our hotel last Tuesday was very useful, and I now have the agreement of my line manager to go ahead with the contract. I am attaching our order as a Word file. Please acknowledge receipt of this email and give us a delivery date.

(d) Further to your last email, I am happy to provide you with the information you need:
On an order for twelve plants we could not give any discount. We believe our prices are very competitive and offer excellent value for money.
Our terms of payment are one month's charges in advance.
Yes, it would be useful to come to the site. Is next Tuesday morning at 10am convenient for you? I can use the opportunity to clarify any other questions that you might have.

(e) I am writing about a visit by one of your maintenance staff earlier today. He left a lot of water on the carpets where he had watered the plants. This was not the high standard of service that we have come to expect from you in the past.

(f) Thanks for your prompt reply. I am interested in obtaining four large plants for our lobby (variety 'Grandifolia') and a further eight for the restaurant area (variety 'Graciosa'). Would you give a discount on an order of this size? Also, can you state your terms of payment as I could not find these on the document you attached? One final thing – do you need to come to the site to see if there is sufficient light? Our address is below.

(g) We are very sorry to hear that the service you received from our company was not up to the usual standard. Unfortunately, a lot of our regular maintenance staff have been ill recently and we had to employ temporary workers. We appreciate the time you have taken to bring this matter to our attention, and as we value our good customer relations, we are willing to give you one week's free maintenance. I apologise again for any inconvenience caused.

(h) It is now 28 days since you accepted delivery of our plants. We attach an invoice for next month's charges. Please pay this asap. Thank you.

Email order: 1 ...*b*... 2 .... 3 .... 4 .... 5 .... 6 .... 7 .... 8 ....

D   Find a word or phrase from the emails which mean:

1   to provide people with something that they need. (email a) ....*supply*...........
2   words or pictures that try to persuade people to buy a product. (email b) ....
3   to tell someone in writing that you have received something. (email c) ....
4   a good relationship between quality (or quantity) and price. (email d) ....
5   a level of quality, skill or ability. (email e) ....
6   the conditions in an agreement or legal document. (email f) ....
7   prepared. (email g) ....
8   the amount of money you have to pay for something. (email h) ....

19 Inquiries and orders

A   Look at the paragraph structure below for two emails: an inquiry (request for information) and the reply. Then write the correct paragraph reference next to each sentence (a–j).

Inquiry
1   How you got the contact.
2   Something about your company, and why you are writing.
3   General request for information.
4   Other specific/unusual questions.
5   Close, perhaps including a reference to future business.

Reply
1   Thanks, referring to the date.
2   Say what you are attaching.
3   Highlight one or two key points.
4   Answer any specific questions.
5   Close, saying you are ready to answer any other questions.

a) We are a distributor of kitchen products in Hungary. We are interested in …   _Inquiry 2_

b) I am attaching our current catalogue and price list as a pdf file.   ....

c) I look forward to an early reply, and am sure that there is a market for your products here in Hungary.   ....

d) Could you also provide details of your delivery times, and whether there is any minimum order.   ....

e) Thank you for your email of 4 June inquiring about our products.   ....

f) You will note that our line of MagicMix food processors is on special offer.   ....

g) Please send us information about your product range, including a price list.   ....

h) We met last Thursday on your stand at the Munich Trade Fair.   ....

i) If you need any further information, please do not hesitate to contact me.   ....

j) We dispatch the goods within 24 hours of a firm order, and for first-time customers our minimum order is €5,000.   ....

B   Put paragraphs (a–e) in the emails below in the correct order. Section A will help you.

> **(a)** We are a Turkish company exporting to the EU, and need a firm of lawyers in France to represent us on some legal matters.
>
> **(b)** In particular, we would like to know your experience in dealing with disputes between companies involved in import/export.
>
> **(c)** I am emailing you off your website, which I found through Google.
>
> **(d)** An early reply would be greatly appreciated.
>
> **(e)** We would be grateful for some information about the legal services that your firm offers.

Paragraph order: 1 ....   2 ....   3 ....   4 ....   5 ....

(a) We feel sure that we will be able to represent your interests here in France. May I suggest that I call you at your convenience to discuss the matter further? Please let me know when would be a convenient time. I look forward to hearing from you soon.

(b) Thank you for your email of 4 December asking for information about our legal services.

(c) You will also note that we have represented several Turkish companies, including one of Turkey's major textile exporters. Naturally, our experience in this field includes resolving contractual disputes.

(d) You will see that we give a list of our recent clients, and that the list includes many well-known company names.

(e) I am attaching a document that gives full details of the range of service we offer.

Paragraph order: 6 .... 7 .... 8 .... 9 .... 10 ....

C **Complete sentences 1–12 with the pairs of words from the box. Check the meaning of any unknown words in a dictionary.**

accept/quotation apologise/inconvenience assure/prompt ~~attached/delay~~ correct/amend discount/repeat dispatched/firm first-time/pre-payment note/records processed/track temporarily/stock would/grateful

1 Please return the _attached_ form asap so that your order can be processed without any _delay_ .

2 We .... be .... if you could supply bank references.

3 Our normal terms for .... customers are 50% ....

4 I have spoken to my line manager, and we are pleased to offer a small .... on this occasion in the hope that it will lead to .... orders.

5 The goods will be .... 3 days from receipt of a .... order.

6 We .... you that your order will have our .... attention.

7 We .... your .... Please ship at the first available opportunity.

8 Your order has been .... You can .... shipping details on our website.

9 We .... from our .... that payment of invoice 5718 is still outstanding.

10 We are .... out of .... of this item, but we expect new supplies shortly.

11 We .... for any .... which may have been caused.

12 The .... information is given below. Please .... your records accordingly.

20 Discussing and agreeing terms

A Match the words (1–8) with the definitions (a–h).

1 discount ....
2 credit ....
3 delivery time ....
4 terms of payment ....
5 minimum order ....
6 guarantee/warranty ....
7 transport costs ....
8 procedure ....

a) the conditions of a sales contract
b) the cost of delivery
c) the smallest number of items that can be supplied
d) a reduction in price
e) how long the goods will take to arrive
f) the correct way of doing something
g) an arrangement to buy goods and pay for them later
h) a promise to repair a product or replace it

Now match the verbs in the columns below with these nouns: *an agreement, a compromise, an offer, an order*. Check any unknown words in a dictionary.

9 cancel/confirm/make/place/receive ....
10 accept/increase/make/reject/withdraw ....
11 keep to/make/negotiate/reach/sign ....
12 accept/agree on/find/reach/suggest ....

B Complete the emails by writing *one* word in each gap. The first letter/s have been given each time to help you.

Email 1

Dear Ms Newman
Thank you for sending your current catalogue and price (1) l *ist*................ last week. We are interested in purchasing 5,000 (2) u................ of product ref TG67 and 2,000 of product ref K800. However, there are one or two things we would like to clarify before going ahead with a firm (3) o................ .
1 Do you give any (4) d................ on an order of this (5) s................ ?
2 Would you be (6) pr................ to let us have the goods on (7) cr................ ? Our normal
   (8) t................ of payment are 60 days after delivery, and we can of course supply a bank
   (9) g................ .
3 We can find no mention of delivery times in your documentation. We need these items by the end of October at the (10) la................ .
If we can (11) r................ an agreement on these matters, we are sure that we can do more business with you in the future. We are a (12) w................ – k................ company that has been in the market for over twenty years.
We look forward to hearing from you soon.
Pavel Witkiewicz

Email 2

Dear Mr Witkiewicz

Thank you for your email of 2 August inquiring about a possible order for our products ref nos. TG67 and K800. I will go through your questions in order.

1 In (13) r_____ to discounts, we would be happy to let you have a discount of 5% on an order of this size.

2 With (14) r_____ to your request for credit, unfortunately, we are not able to offer 60 days credit to (15) fi_____ – t_____ customers. However, I am sure we can find an acceptable (16) com_____ . In view of your reputation in the market, our credit (17) co_____ department will agree on 30 days, with no pre-payment necessary. Our normal (18) pro_____ is to check all bank guarantees, so we will be requiring (19) fu_____ details if you decide to go ahead with your order.

3 Your final question is about delivery times. We can supply the items you require directly from (20) st_____ , and the goods will leave our warehouse within 3 working days of a firm order.

Please also note that we have recently improved the functionality of our website, and it is now possible to (21) pl_____ an order on-line. Alternatively, you can print out the attached order form. Just (22) f_____ it in and return it to us by mail.

I have arranged for a member of our customer services (23) t_____ to give you a call later in the week. They will be able to (24) d_____ with any further points.

Thank you for your interest in our products.

Sylvia Newman

C <u>Underline</u> the correct prepositions in each sentence.

1 Thank you *for/about* your interest in our products.

2 We are interested *in/to* purchasing 5,000 units.

3 Do you give discounts *to/on* an order of this size?

4 We will be happy to deal *to/with* any further questions.

5 Is it possible to buy the goods *on/with* credit?

6 We need these items *until/by* the end of October at the latest.

7 We need to reach agreement *on/for* this matter as soon as possible.

8 We have 20 items *on/in* order from you.

9 Thank you for your email about a possible order *by/for* our products.

10 In relation *with/to* discounts, our terms are 5% for an order over €10,000.

11 We offer a discount *of/by* 5%.

12 With regard to your request *for/of* 60 days credit, unfortunately we are not able to do this.

13 There are one or two things to clarify before going *ahead/in front* with an order.

14 Our company has been *on/in* the market for over forty years.

15 This product has been *on/in* the market for over a year.

16 We are prepared to compromise *at/over* the question of transport costs.

17 We can supply the items you require directly *of/from* stock.

18 The goods will leave our warehouse *within/until* 3 working days of a firm order.

21 Asking for payment

A Make complete sentences by using one phrase from each column. The first one has been done for you.

1 I wish to draw	an overdue payment	to continue.
2 There is	be allowed	to my two previous emails.
3 We are concerned that	your attention	to recover the money.
4 This situation cannot	the matter has not yet	on your account.
5 We must urge you to take	your cooperation	received your attention.
6 We have still not	but to take legal action	the outstanding sum.
7 We shall have no alternative	received payment for	in resolving this matter.
8 We would appreciate	immediate action to	settle your account.

Note: *overdue* and *outstanding* both mean 'not yet paid'; *to settle* means 'to pay the money you owe'.

B Read the emails below. Which email is the:

first reminder .... second reminder .... third reminder .... final demand ....

Email 1

> Following my emails of [DATE/S] I must inform you that we have still not received payment for the outstanding sum of €4,500. Unless we receive payment within seven days we shall have no alternative but to take legal action to recover the money.
> In the meantime, your existing credit facilities have been suspended.

Email 2

> I wish to draw your attention to my previous emails of [DATE/S] about the overdue payment on your account. We are very concerned that the matter has not yet received your attention.
> Clearly, this situation cannot be allowed to continue, and we must urge you to take immediate action to settle your account.

Email 3

> According to our records, the sum of €4,500 is still outstanding on your account.
> We trust that our service was to your satisfaction, and we would appreciate your cooperation in resolving this matter as soon as possible.

Email 4

> On [DATE/S] I wrote to you regarding your company's unpaid account, amounting to €4,500.
> May we please remind you that this amount is still outstanding. We would be grateful to receive a bank transfer in full settlement without further delay.

C Tick (✓) the most polite form, a) or b).

1a) This invoice should be paid immediately. ....

b) You must pay this invoice immediately. ....

2a) You have not paid invoice JK387. ....

b) We note from our records that invoice JK387 has not been paid. ....

3a) This outstanding balance is now overdue. ....

b) Your outstanding balance is now overdue. ....

4a) Please send a bank transfer to clear this amount. ....

b) Please send a bank transfer to clear this amount. If you have already dealt with this matter, then please disregard this email. ....

Note: the first reminder should be polite and impersonal – don't assume your customer has no intention of paying.

D Complete the emails with the phrases from the box.

concerning a payment	forward the payment	further delay	have still not received
now two months overdue	shall have no alternative	should have been cleared	
the outstanding sum	to settle your account		

First reminder

We are writing to you (1)... of €12,600 for invoice number KJ678 which is now overdue. A copy of the invoice is attached.

This amount (2)... by the end of last month. Please send a bank transfer
(3).. , or an explanation of why the balance is still outstanding. If you have already dealt with this matter, please disregard this email.

Second reminder

With reference to my email of 21 March, I must inform you that we (4)...
payment to clear the balance on your account. I am sure you are aware that late payments create problems for us. We would appreciate payment of (5)... without (6)...........................
....

If you have any queries on this matter, please do not hesitate to contact me. Thank you for your cooperation.

Final demand

I wrote to you on 21 March and 7 April regarding the balance of €12,600 on your account. I attach copies of both emails. This sum is (7)... . We are very concerned that the matter has not yet received your attention. Please (8)... within seven days.
If we do not receive payment from you, we (9)... but to take legal action to recover the full amount.

22 Describing business trends

A Review the language of trends.

1 Complete the pairs of opposites with the words from the box.

a) to go up / to ..._go down_...

b) to rise / to ....

c) to improve / to ....

d) to reach a peak / to ....

e) to increase / to ....

f) to grow / to ....

g) to be up / to ....

h) to fluctuate / to ....

be down	fall
be stable	get worse
decrease	~~go down~~
shrink	hit a low

2 Complete these irregular verb forms.

go – we..._nt_.. – g......   rise – ro......... – ri........   grow – gr......... – gr.........   fall – fe......... – fa.........

3 Complete the sentences with one of these words: _gradually, sharply, significantly, slightly, slowly, steadily._

a) Sales increased ..._slowly_... (not fast)

b) Sales increased .... (suddenly)

c) Sales increased .... (a little)

d) Sales increased .... (slowly over a long time)

e) Sales increased .... (noticeably)

f) Sales increased .... (gradually and regularly)

4 Change the verb + adverb form into an adjective + noun form.

to improve gradually ⇨ a grad.............. impro..............   to grow slowly ⇨ sl.............. gro..............

5 Complete the sentences with one of these words: _by, by, for, from, in, of, since, to._

a) Sales increased .... 3%. (_after a verb_)

b) There was an increase .... 3%. (_after a noun and before an amount_)

c) There was a 3% increase .... sales. (_after a noun and before the topic_)

d) Sales increased .... 15,000 .... 17,500 – so they increased .... 2,500.

e) Sales have been increasing .... January (_point in time_) / .... six months (_period of time_).

B <u>Underline</u> the correct words in the email.

Petra – here are the main points from the second quarter results:

At the start of the quarter sales stood (1)_in/at_ $25 million. Then they (2)_rose/rised_ over the three months (3)_to/until_ $27.6 million – an increase (4)_by/of_ around 12%.

It's even better if you look at the year-on-year (5)_quantities/figures_. Last year sales increased (6)_by/with_ only 6% over the same quarter.

The trend is also good for the rest of this year. We're looking at (7)_steady/steadily_ (8)_growing/growth_ going forward.

Congratulations are due to everyone. However, there is a downside. Market share is not growing as fast as sales. In fact, it's been more or less stable (9)_for/since_ the last few years (10)_at/with_ around 18%. In a (11)_rapid/rapidly_ growing market our competitors have benefited as much as us, and in the future we must (12)_to watch/watch_ this very closely.

I look forward to hearing your comments. Regards, Mark

C Review the language of forecasts (what is likely to happen in the future). Complete the table with the words/phrases from the box. Be careful: *two* are not used.

are likely to	could	could not	I expect	I doubt	~~I'm sure~~	may not
might	might not	won't probably	probably won't	won't		

	✓	✗
Definite	Sales will definitely increase. (1) *I'm sure* that sales will increase.	Sales definitely (2) .... increase. I'm certain that sales won't increase.
Probable	(3) .... that sales will increase. Sales (5) .... increase.	Sales (4) .... increase. (6) .... that sales will increase.
Possible	Sales (7) .... increase. Sales (9) .... increase.	Sales (8) .... increase. Sales (10) .... increase.

Now match the verb groups 11–13 with the ends of the sentences a)–c). Be careful!

11 We expect/would like ......   a) to increase sales next year.

12 We expect/would like/hope/intend/plan/want ......   b) sales will increase next year.

13 We expect/think/hope/believe/imagine/predict/forecast ......   c) sales to increase next year.

Note: we can usually use *will* or *going to* to make predictions and there is very little difference. However, if there is strong evidence in the present situation then *going to* is more common.

*I think sales **will** probably increase next year.*   (it's my general belief)

*I think sales **are going to** increase next year.*   (I am looking at some figures right now)

D <u>Underline</u> the correct words or phrases in the email.

Petra – thanks for your comments on the second quarter results. You asked me for my thoughts about the longer term, so here they are:

Sales are (1)*possible/likely* to end this year (2)*with/at* about $34m. I think that profits (3)*to increase/will increase* at an even faster rate, due to our recent cost-cutting measures.

Next year the situation is a lot more (4)*uncertain/unlikely*. This is because of the general economic climate in which we are operating. Inflation (5)*will probably/probably will* start to rise, and I think the Central Bank is planning (6)*interest rates to raise/to raise interest rates* as a result. That's bad news for us. Our debt repayments to the bank are (7)*likely/likely to* go up (8)*considerably/considerable*.

Unemployment is also (9)*to increase/increasing*. Eventually this (10)*might be/might have* an impact on consumer sentiment, although the rate of increase is quite slow and we (11)*probably won't/won't probably* be in such a bad situation as during the last recession.

We can discuss this tomorrow in more detail. I have to leave now – I didn't bring my umbrella and it looks like (12)*it will/it's going to* rain! Mark.

23 Cause, effect, contrast

A Review the language of cause and effect. Complete the sentences with a word from the box.

as	because	due	from	in	of	of	therefore	to	to

Cause ⇨ Effect

1 Our new marketing campaign should *lead* .... / *result* .... / *create* a big increase in sales.

2 Next month we will start a new marketing campaign. *So,* / ...., / *Because of this,* / .... *a result*, we should see a big increase in sales.

Effect ⇦ Cause

3 The big increase in sales last month *resulted* .... / *was a result* .... / *was because* .... / *was due* .... our new marketing campaign.

4 We saw a big increase in sales last month .... *of* / .... *to* our new marketing campaign.

Note: 'We saw a big increase in sales last month **because we had** a new marketing campaign.' (*NOT* ~~because of we had~~ ...)

Note: using *so/such* to express cause

so + adjective (+ *that*):	Our campaign was **so** <u>successful</u> (**that**) we ...
such + noun (+ *that*):	Our campaign was **such** <u>a success</u> (**that**) we ...
such + adjective + noun (+ *that*):	It was **such** <u>a successful campaign</u> (**that**) we ...

B <u>Underline</u> the correct words or phrases in the email.

> Petra, I've had (1)*so/such* a busy week, but finally I've had a chance to talk to Marketing and look at the figures in more detail. Here are our thoughts on the recent trends in sales:
> - The market as a whole is growing, and (2)*as a result/because of* we have benefited along with all our other competitors.
> - However, this fact alone cannot explain why sales are growing (3)*so/such* fast. If you look at the figures you'll see that much of the increase is (4)*due to/result from* the success of just two products, Viva and Avanti. We had a big advertising campaign for Viva before Christmas, which (5)*resulted to/led to* the peak in sales in December. Avanti on the other hand has been selling well throughout the year, probably (6)*because of/because* it already has a good reputation in the market.
> - We must make sure that our new lines are equally successful. (7)*So/As a result of*, someone needs to prepare a detailed marketing plan and circulate it to everyone. Jim should probably deal with this (8)*because of/because* his work on Viva and Avanti. I'll suggest it to him.
> Hope this is helpful, Mark.

C Complete the words in each sentence with the missing letters.

1 Sales increased, **thou** *gh* /**alth** _ _ _ _ market share remained the same.

2 Sales increased, **where** _ _ /**whi** _ _ market share remained the same.

3 Market share remained the same **in sp** _ _ _ **of/des** _ _ _ _ the increase in sales.

4 **In s** _ _ _ _ **of/De** _ _ _ _ _ the increase in sales, market share remained the same.

5 **In spite of the fa** _ _ **th** _ _ sales increased, market share remained the same.

6 Sales increased. **How** _ _ _ _ **,/Ne** _ _ _ _ _ _ _ _ **ss,/E** _ _ **n so**, market share remained the same.

7 **Even th** _ _ _ _ market share remained the same, sales increased.

8 **E** _ _ _ **if** it means reducing prices, we must try to increase market share.

Note:
- Compare *although/though* with *whereas/while*. The first two have a strong sense of surprise; the last two simply compare two facts and emphasise the difference between them.
- *In spite of/despite* + noun phrase, BUT *in spite of the fact that* + subject + verb.
- *However/Nevertheless* are more formal, *Even so* is less formal.
- We can use *even* with *though* and *if* to make a stronger contrast.

D Read the email. Then choose the best word to fill each gap from A, B, C or D below.

> Hiroshi – here's the summary of the market report for East Asia that I promised you.
> - As we all know, last year was a difficult one. (1)....... , since January things (2)....... been getting better. Sales have recovered (3)....... 4% in China, our biggest market. We are (4)....... to see a similar (5)....... in Japan and Korea over the next few quarters, (6)....... right now sales there are (7)....... .
> - In relation to the long term, we are optimistic. Our (8)....... is that economic growth in the whole region (9)....... begin to (10)....... from the start of next year. This will (11)....... labour market and other structural reforms, which in our opinion will take place (12)....... there are some changes in the government. This growth will (13)....... many new opportunities, (14)....... we will face increasing competition from US and other companies.

1) **A** So	**B** Even if	**C** Despite	**D** However
2) **A** have slow	**B** have slowly	**C** are slow	**D** are slowly
3) **A** for	**B** with	**C** by	**D** on
4) **A** possibility	**B** perhaps	**C** possible	**D** likely
5) **A** recover	**B** improve	**C** improvement	**D** growing
6) **A** although	**B** nevertheless	**C** so	**D** as a result of
7) **A** plain	**B** equal	**C** flat	**D** level
8) **A** trend	**B** forecasting	**C** prevision	**D** forecast
9) **A** will	**B** will to	**C** is going	**D** it is possible
10) **A** steadily rise	**B** rise steadily	**C** rising steadily	**D** will rise steadily
11) **A** be due to	**B** result of	**C** be resulted from	**D** because of
12) **A** as a result	**B** whereas	**C** even if	**D** despite
13) **A** create	**B** lead	**C** result to	**D** improve
14) **A** despite	**B** whereas	**C** so	**D** even though

24 Complaints

A Complete the sentences typical of emails of complaint with the pairs of words from the box.

appreciate/replaced   attention/problem   complain/quality   connection/attitude
delivered/urgently   dissatisfaction/received   entitled/replacement   matter/inconvenience
purchased/standard   refund/further   terms/treatment   unless/cancel

1   I am writing in .... with the negative .... of a member of your staff.

2   I hope that you will deal with this .... promptly as it is causing me considerable
    ....

3   The equipment I ordered has still not been ...., despite my phone call to you last
    week to say that it is needed ....

4   Although you advertise yourself as a top-quality brand, the product I .... was well
    below the .... I expected.

5   I am writing to draw your .... to a .... in your customer services section.

6   I would .... it if the faulty goods could be .... as soon as possible.

7   I wish to complain in the strongest possible .... about the .... I received
    from a member of your staff.

8   I believe that I am .... to an immediate ....

9   I am writing to express my strong .... with the goods I .... this morning.

10   .... I receive the goods by the end of this week, I will have no choice but to
    .... my order.

11   I am writing to .... about the .... of a product I purchased on-line from
    your website.

12   I insist on a full ...., otherwise I will be forced to take the matter ....

B Match the beginnings (1–8) with the endings (a–h).

1   You only sent 7 DVDs, instead ....   a) there were only 7 in the box.

2   You only sent 7 DVDs, in spite of ....   b) but there were only 7 in the box.

3   Even though I paid for 8 DVDs, ...   c) However, there were only 7 in the box.

4   I paid for 8 DVDs. ....   d) so I am refusing to pay your invoice.

5   I paid for 8 DVDs, ...   e) Therefore, I am refusing to pay your invoice.

6   Firstly, the quantity of DVDs was incorrect. ....   f) of the 8 that I ordered.

7   You have still not resolved the problem   g) the fact that I paid for 8.
    with the DVDs. ....

         h) In addition, two of the covers were damaged.

8   You have still not resolved the problem
    with the DVDs, ...

C Complete each phrase with *one* word. Some letters have been given to help you.

1 to write in co*nnectio*n with sth.
2 to need sth. *ur*............*y*
3 to take the matter *fu*............*r*
4 to demand a full *re*............*d*
5 to draw sb's *at*............*n* to sth.

6 to be below the expected *st*............*d*
7 to complain in the strongest possible *te*............*s*
8 to express strong *dis*............*ion* with sth.
9 to demand an immediate *repl*............*t*
10 to cause sb. considerable *inc*............*e*

D Linking words and phrases are used in complaints to explain your case clearly and carefully. Complete the table with the words/phrases from the box.

> Above all   As a result   Even though   Finally   Firstly   ~~Furthermore~~   However
> In addition   In conclusion   In fact   In particular   In reality   In spite of the fact that
> Nevertheless   Taking everything into consideration   Therefore

Adding another point (like *and*):	1 *Furthermore* / ....
Listing points:	2 .... / ....
Making a contrast (like *but*):	3 .... / ....
Making a contrast (like *although*):	4 .... / ....
Giving the consequence (like *so*):	5 .... / ....
Giving the most important example:	6 .... / ....
Saying what the real situation is:	7 .... / ....
Introducing the final paragraph:	8 .... / ....

- **Which *two* phrases are NOT followed immediately by a comma, and can come in the middle of a sentence as well as at the beginning?**
.... / ....

E <u>Underline</u> the most appropriate words or phrases in the email.

I am writing to complain about the poor service we have received from your company. (1)*Firstly/Therefore*, the goods you sent were not the ones that we ordered. Our order dated 16 September clearly stated that we wanted 1,000 t-shirts. (2)*In particular/However*, we only received 800. (3)*Nevertheless/Furthermore*, we asked you to print our company logo in the top left corner of the shirts and you have printed it in the centre.
To make matters worse, your staff were very unhelpful when I called. (4)*Even though/Above all*, no-one took responsibility to sort out the problem – I was simply passed from person to person. (5)*In fact/In addition*, after 30 minutes I gave up in frustration and ended the call.
The whole matter was treated by your staff as though it was completely unimportant, (6)*in spite of the fact that/therefore* we have been your customers for more than five years. (7)*In particular/As a result*, we are considering stopping all future business with your company.
(8)*Taking everything into consideration/In reality*, we must insist on an immediate replacement order, to reach here within 14 working days, at no cost to ourselves.

25 Apologies

A Email 1 below is a formal apology, email 2 is an informal apology. Complete the emails by choosing the correct alternatives below. The phrases are in the same order as they appear in the emails.

1/11 ~~for / on behalf of~~

2/12 unprofessional conduct / unfortunate behaviour

3/13 Please accept my sincere apologies for / I'm really sorry for

4/14 You can be sure that / You have my assurance that

5/15 sort out the problem / resolve the matter to your satisfaction

6/16 I'll / We will

7/17 To compensate for the inconvenience caused / As a friendly gesture

8/18 about what happened / regarding the incident

9/19 If you have any further queries / If there's anything else

10/20 please call / do not hesitate to contact me

Email 1: formal

I am writing (1) *on behalf of* Promotional Products in relation to your recent complaint. I was very concerned to learn about the problems you experienced and the (2)... .... of our sales staff. (3).. everything that happened, and thank you for bringing it to my attention. (4)... I will (5)... .
(6).. send replacement items immediately, at our expense, and I will personally make sure that the order is correct. (7).. we will also send you a credit note to be used against any items in our catalogue. I have already spoken to the sales staff involved (8).. and we are making sure that in the future all customer complaints are dealt with in a polite and helpful manner.
Once again, I hope you will accept my apologies for the inconvenience caused. I very much hope you will continue to use our services in the future. (9)... ,
(10).. on my direct line given below.

Email 2: informal

Laura, I'm writing (11) *for* all our family to say thank you very much for letting us stay at your seaside house at the weekend, we really enjoyed it. By now you have probably heard from your neighbours about the (12)... of my teenage son Harry and his friends when they came back from the pub late on Saturday night. (13)... all the noise they made, and for the damage they caused to your neighbour's garden. (14).. .... I will do everything possible to (15).. .
(16).. contact your neighbours directly and offer to pay for any damage. (17)............................ ....I'll also send them them some flowers and a box of chocolates. I've already spoken to my son (18)... and he promises it won't happen again.
Once again, I am really sorry. (19)... ,
(20).. – I'll be at home at the weekend.

B   Match the beginnings of the sentences (1–10) with the endings (a–j).

1   Please accept my ......   a) a replacement immediately.
2   We're having a temporary problem ......   b) and get back to you tomorrow.
3   We're doing everything we can to ......   c) as a gesture of goodwill.
4   Can you leave it ......   d) for any inconvenience this has caused.
5   I'll look into the matter urgently ......   e) hesitate to contact me.
6   I'll send you ......   f) resolve the issue/sort it out.
7   We are sending you a small gift ......   g) sincere apologies.
8   I can assure you that ......   h) this will not happen again.
9   I apologise again ......   i) with me for a day or two?
10 If you have any further queries, do not ......   j) with our software.

Now check the answers, then cover the right hand column and try to remember the endings.

C   Cross out the *one* word or phrase in *italics* in each sentence that is not natural.

1   I am ~~absolutely~~/*extremely*/*really*/*very* sorry for what has happened.
2   Thank you for bringing this *issue/material/matter/problem* to my attention.
3   We can assure you that the *articles/goods/items/wares* were dispatched on time.
4   We were sorry to hear that the product was *damaged/defective/faulty/out of work* when you received it.
5   This was due to *an oversight when we processed your order/a strike in our factory/an inflammation in our warehouse/circumstances beyond our control.*
6   I am trying to *sort it out/sort out it/sort the problem out/sort out the problem* as a matter of urgency.
7   Please return the faulty goods, and we will *refund you/repair them/replace them/restore them* immediately.
8   We appreciate that this has caused you considerable inconvenience, but we cannot accept any *breach in the contract/disadvantage/liability/responsibility* on our part.

D   Rewrite the sentences below with the correct word order.

1   Thank you very much this matter for bringing to my attention.

....

2   I was very experienced to learn the problems about you concerned.

....

3   I will look the matter into and get back you to within the few next days.

....

4   Once again, accept our apologies please caused for the inconvenience.

....

5   Having this matter in detail looked into, I be of no further assistance regret that I can.

....

26 Report structure and key phrases

A Match the different sections of a report (1–5) with their definitions (a–e).

1 Introduction ......   a) The 'body' of the report: a presentation of arguments and evidence.
2 Background ......   b) The subject of the report, who asked for it, why it has been written.
3 Findings ......   c) Practical suggestions for action, often written as a list or bullet points.
4 Conclusion ......   d) The context: what has happened up to now and the general situation.
5 Recommendations ......   e) A judgment or decision based on the discussion in the 'body'.

Note: a report may not have all these sections, and in an email a 'section' may simply be a single sentence.

B Match the beginnings of the sentences (1–12) with the endings (a–l).

1   As requested at the Board meeting ......   a) on the figures sent to me by different departments.
2   The purpose of the report is ......   b) where cost-cutting measures are necessary.
3   The report is based ......   c) in table 1, demand has been falling.
4   I have divided the report ......   d) to suggest ways to reduce costs.
5   As can be seen ......   e) into three sections.
6   This has led to a situation ......   f) of 18 April, here is my report.
7   As mentioned ......   g) the full report and let me have your comments.
8   I suggest that the company ......   h) are as follows:
9   My specific recommendations ......   i) to contact me if you have any questions.
10 Please have a look at ......   j) should be able to cut costs significantly.
11 Your comments will be circulated ......   k) above, sales are going down.
12 Please feel free ......   l) in time for the next meeting.

The order of sentences 1–12 follows (more or less) the order in which they would be used. Write the sentence numbers after these section headings:

Introduction/Background: ....
Findings: ....
Conclusion/Recommendations: ....
Closing comments: ....

C Complete the email with the phrases from the box.

above   as follows   based on the figures   can be seen   divided the report
identify opportunities   I suggest that   investigate the possibility   led to a situation
let me have   make reductions   see section 4.2   purpose of the report   shows that

---

Subject: Cost-cutting measures

As requested at the Board meeting of 18 April, here is my report. The full report is attached as a Word document, but I have written a brief summary below.

Introduction

The (1).. is to suggest ways to reduce costs across the company.

It is (2).. sent to me by different departments last month. I have

(3).. into three sections: background, findings and recommendations.

Background

As (4).. in table 1 in the attached document, demand for our products has

been falling over the last year, and sales and profits are both down. This has (5)..

.... where cost-cutting measures are necessary.

Findings

There are three main areas where cost reductions are possible:

• The marketing budget is very high. As mentioned (6).. , sales are going
  down, but we are still spending large sums on magazine advertising and street posters. This is not
  justified.

• Production costs are also high. Table 2 in the report (7).. raw material
  costs have gone up by 12% over the last year. We must find a way to bring these down.

• We may also have to dismiss a small number of administrative staff, which will be very unpopular.
  (8).. of the full report for suggestions on how to proceed.

Recommendations

In conclusion, (9).. the company should be able to cut costs significantly by

the end of the year. My specific recommendations are (10).. :

1 Marketing Dept to (11).. in the advertising budget of 10% or 15%.

2 Production Dept to (12).. of using different suppliers to bring down
  materials costs.

3 Head Office to (13).. for cutting a limited number of jobs, in case the
  situation deteriorates.

Please have a look at the full report and (14).. your comments by 2 June at
the latest. These will then be circulated to all departmental managers in time for the meeting on 16 June.
Please feel free to contact me if you have any questions.

27 Linking words and relative clauses

A **First, read the information about linking words and phrases. Then read through the email and <u>underline</u> 18 linking words/phrases in it, not including 'and', 'but' and 'or'.**

Linking words and phrases join one idea to another. They help the reader to understand the structure of your argument. There are two types:

- Words in the middle of a sentence that join two clauses: *and, but, because, so* etc.
- Words/phrases at the beginning of a sentence: *However, Therefore, In relation to* etc. These are often followed by a comma.

Subject: Arrangements for sales conference
Marcia – many thanks for sending the details of the 165 participants coming to our sales conference in November. Here is my report on the arrangements that will be necessary.

1 <u>Accommodation</u>
In previous years we have used the Belmont Hotel. <u>In general</u>, we have always had good feedback from delegates on the Belmont. However, it is quite far from the conference centre, and in addition they have increased their prices recently. As a result, I am going to get an alternative quote from the York Hotel this year.

2 <u>Conference Centre</u>
In relation to numbers, the hall seats 200 people, so there shouldn't be any problem. Nevertheless, if we get a lot of late bookings we may need a bigger hall. I will monitor the situation closely. Obviously, if people book after the deadline we may have to write back and say we are full.
On another point, we need to make sure that the amplification system is working properly, as last year several delegates complained that the sound was too low at the back of the hall.

3 <u>Speakers</u>
Both outside speakers are confirmed. In particular, the well-known author Sandra Brett has agreed to give a talk on 'Motivation', and I'm sure it will be very well received.

4 <u>Food and drink</u>
Last year this was a problem. Firstly, we had a lot of complaints about the food. Secondly, there was some confusion among delegates about whether they should stay in the conference centre for lunch or go outside. In fact, if delegates do want to go outside and get some fresh air it is not a problem. So this year I am going to get quotes from catering companies for two options, that is to say one for coffee breaks and snacks only, and the other for lunch as well. Alternatively, we could just use the café in the conference centre and not employ an outside firm, but I don't think that will create a good impression.

I think that's all. Let me know if there's anything else, especially if you suddenly get a lot of late bookings.
Bruno

B Complete the table with the words from the boxes.

> Alternatively   e.g.   ~~Finally~~   For instance   Instead of   Moreover   Nevertheless
> On another point   On the other hand   On the whole   ~~Secondly~~   Usually

Showing a sequence:	*Firstly*	1	*Secondly*	2	*Finally*
Talking generally:	*In general*	3		4	
Making a contrast:	*However*	5		6	
Adding another point:	*In addition*	7		8	
Giving an example:	*For example*	9		10	
Giving an alternative:	*Either … or …*	11		12	

> Above all   Actually   As a matter of fact   For this reason   i.e.   In particular
> Obviously   Of course   Regarding   That is to say   Therefore   With reference to

Saying what the real situation is:	*In fact*	13		14	
Saying something is obvious:	*Clearly*	15		16	
Giving the most important point:	*Especially*	17		18	
Rephrasing in a different way:	*In other words*	19		20	
Giving a result/consequence:	*As a result*	21		22	
Introducing a new topic:	*In relation to*	23		24	

Note: you can find more practice with linking words in units 23, 24 and 30.

C Rewrite each pair of sentences as one sentence, including the word in brackets. Begin as shown, and make any necessary changes.

1   The Board issued a report. It describes options for our long-term strategy. (**that**)
The report *that the Board issued describes options for our long-term strategy.*

2   The Board issued a report. It describes options for our long-term strategy. (**which**)
The Board *issued a report which describes options for our long-term strategy.*

3   We interviewed three candidates. They were all very good. (**who**)
We interviewed ....

4   We interviewed three candidates. They were all very good. (**that**)
The three ....

5   Marketing want to postpone the product launch. I feel this is a mistake. (**which**)
Marketing want ....

6   We might need to dismiss some workers. These workers are listed below. (**who**)
The workers ....

7   One team's results were particularly good. This team should be given a bonus. (**whose**)
The team ....

28 Being direct and brief

A Look at the differences in style between these two emails. Notice how version 2 uses the key words (<u>underlined</u>) from version 1. The form of the words may be different.

Version 1

> Subject: My ideas following last Friday's meeting
> In the attached Word document you'll find my thoughts about the marketing plan that we discussed in <u>last</u> Friday's <u>meeting</u>, and in particular my response to Jenny's points about <u>needing a new type of packaging</u> to appeal to a younger age group. I think she raised some important issues, and so I'm circulating these <u>ideas</u> to everyone who was present at the meeting. <u>Please</u> insert your <u>comments</u> in the <u>attached document</u> and email it back to me <u>as soon as possible</u>.

Version 2

> Subject: Ideas for packaging
> We need a new type of packaging – as we all agreed in the last meeting. My ideas are in the attached document. Comments please asap.

Match the descriptions (1–6) below by <u>underlining</u> the most appropriate version, 1 or 2.

1 The email is direct and brief.   *Version 1/2*
2 The email is friendly and shows more respect to the reader.   *Version 1/2*
3 The action required is very clear.   *Version 1/2*
4 The exact action required is not so clear.   *Version 1/2*
5 Unless the reader knows the writer well, the email could sound a bit aggressive.   *Version 1/2*
6 There may be too much in the email to write in a busy working day.   *Version 1/2*

B Rewrite the email below. The maximum length is **50 words**, including the subject line. Some key words have been <u>underlined</u> to help you, but you may need to change their form.

> Subject: Confirmation of our meeting as discussed by phone
> I'm writing regarding <u>our phone call</u> earlier this morning. It was a very useful discussion and I am much clearer now about your objectives. At the end of the call you suggested a time and place for our next <u>meeting</u>, the <u>lobby of the Intercontinental Hotel in Barcelona</u> at <u>2.00</u> pm <u>on 7th February</u>. I believe you will be staying at the hotel at that time. I said that I would email you to confirm the meeting. Well, for me the time and place is very good – I am free all afternoon. I <u>look forward to seeing you there</u> at that time and I hope that in the evening you can <u>be my guest for dinner</u> at a good restaurant in Barcelona.

Subject: ....

....

....

....

C Cross out 20 words which are not necessary in this email.

> Many thanks for your email which I received yesterday. Tuesday at 10.30 is fine for me as my 9am meeting will be finished by then. Can you send me the latest sales figures before the meeting? I look forward to seeing you there.

D Cross out 20 words which are not necessary in this email.

> I am writing to all my colleagues to let you know that I will be away from my office from 14–21 November on a visit to Hungary. Please direct all questions that you have to Helga in my absence.

E <u>Underline</u> the key words then rewrite the email. The maximum length is **60 words**, including the subject line.

> Subject: Your info re market developments in the Baltic States
> Many thanks for getting in touch last week and sending me all the information about market changes in the Baltic States. It was really useful, particularly the graphs about expected demand for consumer products over the next five years. I've forwarded your email to our representative in Estonia, Krista Kilvet. She has just taken over from Doris Kareva, who I think you met in Stuttgart. Would you be interested in giving a presentation at our Head Office on the whole political and economic background in the region? I'm sure the Board would be interested as we may be making some large investments there in the near future.

Subject: ....

....

....

....

....

F <u>Underline</u> the key words then rewrite the email. The maximum length is **60 words**, including the subject line.

> Subject: Thank you for your help at the conference in London
> Thank you so much for all your help during the conference on the future of the airline industry that I attended in London last week. Your help was really appreciated as I had never been to the UK before and everything was very new to me! The conference was really interesting. Of course, while I was there I also had the great pleasure to meet your UK sales team. They are a wonderful group of people and I would like you to give my best regards to all of them. As you know, there are plans to bring some of the UK staff over here to Dubai at the end of the year to see how we run the Dubai office. I look forward to seeing you then.

Subject: ....

....

....

....

....

29 Being indirect and polite

A The short phrases in the table below use standard/neutral language. Complete the table with the polite/diplomatic phrases from the box.

> ~~Could you possibly~~   Do you need any help with   Is it all right if I   I was wondering if you could
> I wonder if I could   Perhaps we should   Why don't we   Would you like me to

Requests (asking somebody else)
Can/Could you … ?   1 *Could you possibly* / .... ?
Permission (for yourself)
Can/Could I … ?   2 .... / .... ?
Offering help
Can I/Shall I … ?   3 .... / .... ?
Suggestions
What about (+ -ing)/Shall we …? 4 .... / .... ?

B Here are more ways to make your language polite/diplomatic. Complete the words in each sentence with the missing letters.

There will be a delay.	⇨	1 I'm af *r a i d* there will be a sm _ _ _ delay.
There is a problem.	⇨	2 It se _ _ _ we have a sl _ _ _ _ problem.
I disagree.	⇨	3 I th _ _ _ there m _ _ be an issue here.
We can't do that.	⇨	4 To be ho _ _ _ _, I'm not s _ _ _ we can do that.
That gives us very little time.	⇨	5 Act _ _ _ _ _ _, that does _' _ give us m _ _ _ time.
It will be better to ask Heidi.	⇨	6 Wou _ _ _ ' _ it be better to ask Heidi?
That will be very expensive.	⇨	7 That mi _ _ _ be qu _ _ _ expensive.
That will be very expensive	⇨	8 That won' _ be ch _ _ _ .

C Rewrite each sentence with the words in brackets to make them more polite and diplomatic.

1 Can we meet again next week? (wonder/could) ....
2 You've made a mistake on the invoice. (there/seems) ....
3 The quality is low. (not very) ....
4 Shall I speak to Mr Baker? (would you like) ....
5 Your estimate for the cost is too low. (might/a bit) ....
6 We should wait. (wouldn't/better idea) ....
7 It's a bad idea. (honest/I'm not sure/good) ....
8 Let's cancel the project. (perhaps/should think about) ....

D   **Read the situation. Then complete the words in each reply with the missing letters.**

Somebody sends you an email: *I've just had a great idea! We could have a team meeting every Monday morning at 8am to plan the week's work.* You want to disagree:

1   It sou *nds* like a good idea, but I'm not sure it would work in pra............. .
2   I can see what you're sa............. , but wh............. a............. the traffic on Monday mornings?
3   Wo............'............. some people find that a li............. early?
4   To be ho............. , I'm not s............. that would be conv............. for everybody.
5   I know what you m............. , but I can see one or two problems with that.
6   It's a good idea, but d............'............. you think 9am wo............. be b............r?

Look back at sentences (1–6) and find:

a)   four examples of *Yes, but …* .... /......... /......... /.........
b)   a normal question to show doubt ....
c)   two negative questions to show doubt .... /.........
d)   an introductory phrase to prepare the reader for disagreement ....

E   **Make the emails below more polite or diplomatic by changing the words in *italics*. Use techniques from sections A–C.**

Luisa, thanks for your email about the new brochure and the attached file with the quote from the printers. [1]*It is* [2]*very* expensive. [3]*Isn't it* a better idea to contact some other printing firms and get some alternative quotes? After all, [4]*we have been very unhappy* with the quality of their work on the last few jobs. What do you think?

1   *It seems / I think it's*   3 ....
2   ....   4 ....

Frank – sorry we didn't have a chance to talk yesterday. Actually, I have [5]*a favour* to ask. [6]*I wonder if you can* have a word with Sandra in Human Resources about when the position of Sales Director is going to be advertised. [7]*It's delicate* for me, as I'm sure you understand, because there is a chance [8]*I will be* one of the candidates. Thanks.

5   ....   7 ....
6   ....   8 ....

Steven, thanks for sending the suggestions on how to price our new range of accessories. [9]*I don't agree* with you. The prices you suggest [10]*are* [11]*too* high for the market. Don't you think a lower price [12]*will* result in higher sales and therefore higher profits? Let me know what you think.

9   ....   11 ....
10   ....   12 ....

30 Being friendly

A There are many words and phrases that you can use at the beginning of a sentence to sound friendly. Complete the table with the words or phrases from the box below.

Anyway	Apparently	Basically	By the way	Frankly	In fact	Luckily	Of course

You heard something, but are not sure:	*It seems that*	1	....
Something is true, but surprising:	*Actually*	2	....
Something is obvious or already known:	*Obviously*	3	....
Bad /good fortune:	*Unfortunately*	4	....
Saying what you really think:	*To be honest*	5	....
Going back to a topic:	*Well/So*	6	....
Changing the topic:	*Anyway/So*	7	....
Summarising with the most important point:	*Anyway*	8	....

B Complete the email with words or phrases from section A. Several answers may be possible. There is one solution that uses each line in the table above just once.

Hi, I'm just back from India – I had a fantastic time. (1)................................... , it's probably one of the best holidays I've ever had. Did you get the email I sent from Delhi? I didn't have much time to write because it was late and the owner of the Internet café wanted to close up for the night. (2)................................... , he kept it open for a few more minutes so I could finish emailing. (3)................................... , as I was saying, I really enjoyed myself. I went to Agra to see the Taj Mahal, and I also went to an amazing wildlife reserve called Sariska. (4)................................... , I did have the usual stomach problems at the beginning of the trip, but nothing too bad. (5)................................... , have you heard the news about Anoushka? (6)................................... , she's just met a guy she really likes and they're getting married next year! His name is Walter. She's only known him for a month. Sara says she met him at a party last week but he didn't seem very friendly. (7)................................... , I always thought Anoushka rushed into things too quickly. What do you think? Don't you think she's a bit young to get married? (8)................................... , it's her decision at the end of the day. That's all for now. Hope to hear from you soon. Bye!

Note:
- The words in the gaps make the email sound friendly. Try reading it without these words – it still makes sense, but it is too direct.
- The words in the gaps can help to make the email easier to follow. They show the structure of the text, how the writer is going to continue.
- The words in the gaps are followed by a comma in writing. This is like pausing in speech.

C Read the email below twice. The second time you read it, miss out all the words underlined. What is the difference?

> Hi Patti! Thanks for your email. Your new job sounds <u>really</u> great – <u>I know that</u> you've wanted to work as a graphic designer for ages <u>and ages,</u> <u>and now it's finally happened! Congratulations! I'm sure you'll do really well in the job. Well,</u> what about my news? I arrived in Prague about a month ago. <u>It was quite difficult at first. Of course</u> I couldn't speak the language, and finding a place to live wasn't easy. Then my friend Belen and I found a <u>lovely little</u> flat <u>in the old part of town</u>. It's <u>quite</u> small, <u>but it's full of character and we love it</u>. I'm working as a waitress <u>in a cocktail bar</u>. It's okay – <u>I don't suppose I'll do it for long, but</u> it's a way to earn some money. <u>Anyway, that's all for now</u>. I hope you're well, and give my regards to your family – especially your mother. <u>She was so kind to me when I came and stayed at your house</u>. All the best, Florencia.

Check your answer in the Answer key at the back of the book.

D Rewrite the email with the words and phrases from the box to make it more friendly. Some of the words and phrases like *really, to be honest* and *First* can go in several places. You may also need to change the punctuation in places.

First,	really	a bit	hundreds of	a few lines	all day long	to be honest

as you probably know,　　Oh well, that's life!　　the next thing is　　she told me last month

Anyway, that's all for now　　but writing to you has helped　　because I'm sure you'll have great fun

Things have been a bit difficult recently.　　but I think it's best for both of us

> Stefan, just to let you know that I can't join you next weekend. I'm sorry, but I've already arranged to go to Paris. I'm staying with Bernard in his flat, and I really need a break. I've broken up with Rosanna. We've been having a lot of arguments recently, and she's going to move to Hamburg. It's a pity. Then, my job. I have a lot of responsibilities in the office and it's quite stressful. We have customers who call and I never get a break. I'm sorry if I sound depressed. Hope to see you soon. All the best, Wilhelm.

....
....
....
....
....
....
....
....
....
....
....
....

31 Advice and suggestions

A Read the email exchange between two friends, then match the phrases in *italics* (1–10) with the phrases (a–j) below.

Hi Toby

Hope you're well.

(1)*I've got a bit of a problem, and I'd really like your advice.* You know I'm doing that secretarial course. Well, it's really boring and I hate it. I've already paid for the course and it runs till the end of June. (2)*Do you have any ideas about* what I should do? (3)*Please email me, or give me a call when you get the chance.*

Sandra

Hi Sandra

(4) *I'm sorry you're having such a hard time at the moment,* but (5) *I think you should* finish the course as you've only got a few months to go. You could concentrate on increasing your typing speed – that's always useful.

Toby

Toby – no, I really hate the course and I don't think I can last till the end of June. (6)*What should I do?*

Sandra

Well, (7)*what about* going to a careers advice centre then? Or doing something really different, like travelling abroad for a year. (8)*That way,* you could be thinking about what you really want to do with your life. (9)*I think it's better than* just giving up the course and doing nothing.

(10)*I hope I've helped a bit.*

Toby

Great idea, Toby! Thanks. I'm off to the travel agent's right now.

Sandra

---

a) I would really appreciate it if you could write back or telephone me to discuss this matter further, at your convenience. *3*

b) I think it might be a good idea to … ……

c) I was wondering if you had any ideas about … ……

d) Have you thought of … (+ *-ing*) ……

e) I'd like your advice about a problem I have. ……

f) I hope I have been of some help. ……

g) I think this option would be preferable to … (+ *-ing*) ……

h) I was sorry to hear about your current difficulties. ……

i) This would mean that … ……

j) What would you advise me to do? ……

- **In general, do you think phrases a)–j) are more formal or more informal than those in the emails?**

B Each phrase below has two words the wrong way round. Correct the mistakes ~~this~~ ~~like~~.

Asking for advice

Opening:	1	I've got a bit of a problem, and maybe can you help.
Asking for advice:	2	I was wondering if you had any ideas about what should I do.
Closing:	3	Please write and let know me what you think.

Giving advice

Opening:	4	I'm sorry you're having a such hard time at the moment.
Giving advice:	5	I think might it be a good idea to finish the course.
Result:	6	This would mean that could you think about what to do next.
Options:	7	I think this option would preferable be to just giving up the course.
Closing:	8	I hope have I been of some help.

C Match the beginnings of the sentences (1–14) with the endings (a–k).

Making a suggestion

1 I think we should ......
2 I suggest ......
3 Shall we ......
4 I think we ought ......
5 Perhaps we could ......
6 How about ......
7 Why don't we ......
8 Let's ......

a) go to an Italian restaurant for your birthday.
b) go to an Italian restaurant for your birthday? (*a question*)
c) to go to an Italian restaurant for your birthday.
d) going to an Italian restaurant for your birthday.
e) going to an Italian restaurant for your birthday? (*a question*)

Accepting/Rejecting a suggestion

9 It's a ......
10 It might be ......
11 I think your idea would ......
12 I'm not so ......
13 It sounds like a good idea, but I don't ......
14 It sounds like a good idea, but I can ......

f) work really well.
g) see one or two problems.
h) great idea!
i) think it would work in practice.
j) worth trying.
k) sure about your idea.

D Complete the sentences by writing *one* word in each gap.

1 I was .... if you .... give me some advice.
2 Please email me when you .... a chance. I'd really .... it.
3 I think you .... finish the course. It's .... than just giving up.
4 What .... going to a careers centre as well? It .... be a good idea.
5 .... we meet up for lunch one day next week to talk .... it?
6 I'm not sure your idea will .... , but it's definitely .... trying.

32 Job application

A Put the parts below into the correct order to make a complete email for someone applying for a job.

(a) the summer programme where I worked last year. I am available for interview in Naples any weekday afternoon, and you can email

(b) as a Word document. You will notice that I have supervised children on a range of sports and cultural activities as well as dealing

(c) Dear Sir/Madam // With reference to your advertisement on the JobFinders.com website, I am interested in applying

(d) as I enjoy working with young people. I have a lot of energy and enthusiasm and am also responsible and reliable. I have attached my CV

(e) First Certificate grade A. I would be grateful if you would consider my application. You will see

(f) the travel industry. During the last few summer holidays I have

(g) for the post of tour leader for Italian school students. I am 26 years old and am currently studying

(h) me or telephone me on the number below. I look forward to hearing from you soon. Yours faithfully

(i) for a diploma in Tourism at Naples University. After that I hope to follow a career in

(j) in the job of tour leader, taking students to London. I feel that I would be well-suited for this job

(k) to do something more varied and challenging, and for this reason I am interested

(l) with transport arrangements and tickets. You will also notice that my English is good and I have

(m) from my attached CV that two people can be contacted as references, one is a university professor and the other is from

(n) worked as a youth leader in Italy, and I enjoyed the work very much. Next summer I would like

1 ..c.. 2 .... 3 .... 4 .... 5 .... 6 .... 7 .... 8 .... 9 ....
10 .... 11 .... 12 .... 13 .... 14 ....

B The email in section A on the previous page is one long paragraph. Show where new paragraphs could begin by writing a // symbol in the text. The structure below will help you.

1 Greeting
2 Reason for writing

For example: where (and when) you saw the advertisement and which job you are interested in.

3 Your background and experience

For example: your age (optional); present job and/or studies; your qualifications (or if you are a student what you hope to do in the future); a description of your recent work experience.

4 The job

For example: mention the skills and personal qualities that make you suitable for this job.

5 Refer to you CV

Ask the reader to look at your CV/Resume, and focus on one or two key points.

6 Final comments

For example: say that you hope your application will be considered; say who will give you a reference; say when you are available for interview; say how you can be contacted.

7 Standard final sentence
8 Formal ending

C Complete the sentences with *one* of these words: *as, at, for, from, in, of, on, to.*

1 With reference .... your advertisement .... the JobFinders.com website, I am interested .... applying .... the post of tour leader.

2 I have attached my CV .... a Word document.

3 I am available .... interview .... Naples.

4 I'm working .... a sales representative at the moment.

5 You can email me or telephone me .... the number given .... my CV.

6 I look forward .... hearing .... you soon.

7 I have a good knowledge .... business administration. I studied it .... university.

8 I'm unemployed .... the moment. I've been out .... work since the summer.

9 I'm studying .... a degree .... Environmental Studies.

10 I hope to follow a career .... the legal profession.

11 I have been working .... Telekom for one year.

12 I attach my CV .... requested.

Phrase bank index

Basics

	Formal/Neutral	Informal
Name	Dear Mr/Mrs/Ms Dupuis Dear Mary	Hi/Hello Mary Mary, … (*or no name at all*)

Previous contact	Thank you for your email of …
	 Further to your last email, …
	 I apologise for not getting in
	    contact with you before now.
		Thanks for your email.
		 Re your email, …
		 Sorry I haven't written for ages,
		    but I've been really busy.

Reason for writing	I am writing in connection with … I am writing with regard to … In reply to your email, here are … Your name was given to me by … We would like to point out that …	Just a short note about … I'm writing about … Here's the … you wanted. I got your name from … Please note that …
Giving information	I'm writing to let you know that … We are able to confirm that … I am delighted to tell you that … We regret to inform you that …	Just a note to say … We can confirm that … Good news! Unfortunately, …
Attachments	Please find attached my report. I'm sending you … as a pdf file.	I've attached … Here is the … you wanted.
Asking for information	Could you give me some information about … I would like to know … I'm interested in receiving/finding out …	Can you tell me a little more about … I'd like to know … Please send me …
Requests	I'd be grateful if you could … I wonder if you could … Do you think I could have …? Thank you in advance for your help in this matter.	Please could you … Could you …? Can I have …? I'd appreciate your help on this.
Promising action	I will … I'll investigate the matter. I will contact you again shortly.	I'll … I'll look into it. I'll get back to you soon.
Offering help	Would you like me to …? If you wish, I would be happy to … Let me know whether you would like me to …	Do you want me to …? Shall I …? Let me know if you'd like me to …

Final comments	Thank you for your help.
	 Do not hesitate to contact us again if you
	    require any further information.
	 Please feel free to contact me if you have
	    any questions. My direct line is …
		Thanks again for …
		 Let me know if you need anything
		    else.
		 Just give me a call if you have
		    any questions. My number is …

Close	I am looking forward to … (+ *-ing*) Give my regards to … Best wishes Regards	Looking forward to … (+ *-ing*) Best wishes to … Speak to/See you soon. Bye (for now)/All the best

Negotiating a project

Asking for information	What are your usual charges (fees/rates) for …? Can you give me some more information about …?
Requests	Do you think you could …? Would you be able to …?
Emphasising a main point	My main concern at this stage is … The main thing for me is …
Asking for a suggestion	How do you think we should deal with this? What do you think is the best way forward?
Making a suggestion	Why don't you …? What about if we …?
Negotiating: being firm	I understand what you're saying about … (but …) I can see what you're saying, but …
Negotiating: being flexible	We would be prepared to … (if …) I am willing to … (if …)
Negotiating: agreeing	Okay, I'm happy with that for now. That's fine.
Next steps	I'll be in touch again soon with more details. Let's talk next week and see how things are going.
Closing	I look forward to working with you. I'm sorry that we couldn't use your services this time, but I hope there will be another opportunity.

Checking understanding

Technical problems	Did you get my last message sent on …? Sorry, you forgot to attach the file. Can you send it again? I got your email, but I can't open the attachment. Did you mean to send this? I don't want to open it in case it's got a virus.
Asking for clarification	I'm not sure what you mean by …? Could you clarify? Which … do you mean? I don't understand this point. Can you explain in a little more detail? Are you sure about that?
Giving clarification	Sorry, what I meant was …, not … I thought …, but I may be wrong. I'll check and get back to you. The correct information is given below. Please amend your records accordingly. Sorry, forget my last email. You're right.
Close	I hope this clarifies the situation. Get back to me if there's anything else.

Arrangements

Meetings

	Formal/Neutral	Informal
Reason for writing	I'm writing to arrange a time for our meeting. What time would be convenient for you?	Just a quick note to arrange a time to meet. When would suit you?
Suggesting time/place	Could we meet on (day) in (the morning etc.) at (time)?	How about (day) at (time)? Are you free sometime next week?
Saying when you are/ are not free	I would be able to attend the meeting on Thursday morning. I'm out of the office until 2pm. Any time after that would be fine. I'm afraid I can't manage next Monday.	I'm free Thursday am. I won't be around until after lunch. Any time after that is okay. Sorry, can't make it next Monday.
Confirming	I'd like to confirm … That's fine. I will call/email you tomorrow to confirm the details.	Thursday is good for me. That should be okay. I'll get back to you if there's a problem.
Changing arrangements	This is to let you know that I will not be able to attend the meeting next Thursday. I wonder if we could move it to …? I apologise for any inconvenience caused.	Re our meeting next week, I'm afraid I can't make Thursday. How about … instead? Sorry for the inconvenience.
Close	I look forward to meeting you in Brussels. Let me know if you need to change the arrangements.	See you in Brussels. Give me a call if anything changes.

Invitations

	Formal/Neutral	Informal
Inviting	We would be very pleased if you could come to … I would like to invite you to … / attend our … Please let me know if you will be able to attend.	I'm writing to invite you to … Would you like to come to …? Please let me know if you can make it.
Prepare	Before the meeting it would be useful if you could prepare … It would be helpful if you could bring …	Please prepare … before the meeting. Please bring to the meeting …
Accepting	Thank you for your kind invitation. The date you suggest is fine. I would be delighted to attend the meeting. I am sure it will be very useful.	Thanks a lot for the invitation. The date's fine for me. I'd love to come to the meeting. It sounds like a great idea.
Refusing	Thank you for your kind invitation. Unfortunately, I have another appointment on that day. Please accept my apologies. I hope we will have the opportunity to meet on another occasion in the near future. I am sure that the meeting will be a great success.	Thanks a lot for your kind invitation. Unfortunately, I have something else in my schedule on that day. I hope we can meet up soon. Good luck with the meeting!

Writing styles

Formal/Informal

	Formal/Neutral	Informal
Example phrases	Thank you for your email received 12 Feb.	Thanks for the email.
	With regard/reference to …	Re …
	I would be grateful if you could …	Please could you …
	We regret to advise you that …	I'm sorry to tell you that …
	Please accept our apologies for …	I'm sorry for …
	I was wondering if you could …	Could you …?
	We note that you have not …	You haven't …
	We would like to remind you that …	Don't forget that …
	It is necessary for me to …	I need to …
	It is possible that I will …	I might …
	Would you like me to …?	Shall I …?
	However, … / In addition, … / Therefore, …	But, … / Also, … / So, …
	If you require any further information, please do not hesitate to contact me.	If you'd like more details, let me know.
	I look forward to meeting you next week.	See you next week.
Latin / Anglosaxon origin	assistance/due to/enquire/inform/information obtain/occupation/possess/provide/repair request/requirements/verify	help/because of/ask/tell/facts get/job/have/give/fix ask for/needs/check (prove)

Direct/Indirect

	Direct	Indirect: polite/diplomatic
Requests	Can you …?	Could you …?
	Please could you …	I was wondering if you could …
Asking for permission	Can I …?	Is it all right if I …?
	Could I …?	I wonder if I could …?
Offering help	Can I …?	Would you like me to …?
	Shall I …?	Do you need any help with …?
Making a suggestion	What about … (+ -ing)?	Why don't we …?
	Shall we …?	Perhaps we should …?
Softening a strong comment	There is a problem.	I'm afraid there is a small problem.
		It seems there is a slight problem.
	That will be very expensive.	That might be quite expensive.
		Won't that be a bit expensive?
	We can't do that.	I'm not sure we can do that.
	That gives us very little time.	Actually, that doesn't give us much time.
	It will be better to ask Heidi.	Wouldn't it be better to ask Heidi?
	I disagree.	I can see what you're saying, but …
		Don't you think that …?
		To be honest, I think it might be better to …

Commercial

Request for information (customer)

Saying how you got the contact	We met last Thursday on your stand at the Munich Trade Fair. I am emailing you off your website, which I found through Google.
Giving reason for writing	We are a manufacturer/supplier/provider of … . We are interested in … We are a Turkish company exporting to the EU, and we need …
General requests	We would be grateful for some information about … Please send us information about your product range and prices.
Specific requests	In particular, we would like to know … Please send full details of your prices, discounts, terms of payment and delivery times. Could you also say whether there is any minimum order.
Close	An early reply would be greatly appreciated. I look forward to an early reply, and am sure that there is a market for your products here in Hungary.

Giving information (supplier)

Thanks	Thank you for your email of 4 June inquiring about …
Giving factual information	We can quote you a price of … CIF/FOB Istanbul. We can deliver by … (date) / within … (period of time) The goods will be shipped 3 days from receipt of a firm order. We can offer a discount of … on orders over … . We require payment by bank transfer/letter of credit. Our normal procedure is to … Our normal terms for first-time customers are … We can supply the items you require directly from stock.
Saying what you are attaching	I am attaching a document that gives full details of … I am attaching our current catalogue and price list as a pdf file.
Highlighting one or two key points	You will see that … You will note that our line of … is on special offer.
Answering specific questions	You will also note that … . Our experience in this field includes … We dispatch the goods within 24 hours of a firm order, and for first-time customers our minimum order is €1,000. I am afraid that model is no longer available. However, …
Close	We feel sure that … . May I suggest that I call you at your convenience to discuss the matter further? If you need any further information, please do not hesitate to contact me. My direct line is …

Following up a call (supplier)

Open	Thank you for taking the time on the telephone this morning to explain … .
Summarising key points	I understand that you are looking for … and I am confident that we can find a good solution for your needs.
Giving additional information	I have attached some information about our company, including … I have attached a list of some of our clients, which you will see include …
Saying you will call back	As agreed, I'll give you a call during the last week of September. I have made a note to call you again after you've had a chance to … Perhaps then it would be a good idea to meet to discuss …
Close	In the meantime, if you would like to discuss any other points, please don't hesitate to give me a call on my direct line … .

Asking for better terms (customer)

Open	Thank you for sending … . We are interested in … . However, there are one or two things we would like to clarify before going ahead.
Discussing terms	Do you give any discount on an order of this size? Would you be prepared to let us have the goods on credit? We need these items by … at the latest.
Close	If we can reach an agreement on these matters we are sure that we can do more business with you in the future. We look forward to hearing from you soon.

Replying and agreeing terms (supplier)

Open	Thank you for your email of … inquiring about a possible order for … .
Saying yes	In relation to …, we would be happy to let you have … I have spoken to my line manager, and we are able to … on this occasion.
Looking for a compromise	With regard to …, unfortunately we are not able to … . However, I am sure we can find an acceptable compromise. We are prepared to accept … .
Final details	We would be grateful if you could supply bank references. Please return the attached form asap so that your order can be processed without any delay. Please note that we have recently improved the functionality of our website, and it is now possible to place an order on-line. Alternatively, you can print out the attached order form and return it to us by mail.
Close	I have arranged for a member of our customer services team to give you a call later in the week. They will be able to deal with any further points. We hope you find our quotation satisfactory and look forward to receiving your order. We assure you that it will have our prompt attention. If you need any further information, do not hesitate to contact us.

Making an order (customer)

Open
Thank you for your recent email, and we accept your quotation. Our completed order form is attached, and we give full bank details below.

Close
Please acknowledge receipt of this order.

Confirming an order (supplier)

Open
Your order has been received.
We can confirm that your goods have been shipped.
You can track shipping details on our website.
Due to exceptional demand these items are temporarily out of stock. We hope to be able to ship your order within … days and will keep you fully informed. We apologise for any inconvenience this may cause.

Close
We are confident that the goods will meet your expectations. Should there be any questions, please do not hesitate to contact me, either by email or phone.

Asking for payment (supplier)

First reminder – open
We are writing concerning a payment of €12,600 for invoice number KJ678 which is now overdue. A copy of the invoice is attached.
According to our records, the sum of €4,500 is still outstanding on your account.

First reminder – action
Please send a bank transfer to settle the account, or an explanation of why the balance is still outstanding. If you have already dealt with this matter, please disregard this email.
We would appreciate your cooperation in resolving this matter as soon as possible.

Second/Third reminder – open
On (date) I wrote to you regarding your company's unpaid account, amounting to €4,500. May we please remind you that this amount is still outstanding.
I wish to draw your attention to my previous emails of (dates) about the overdue payment on your account. We are very concerned that the matter has not yet received your attention.

Second/Third reminder – action
We need a bank transfer in full settlement without further delay.
Clearly, this situation cannot be allowed to continue, and we must ask you to take immediate action to settle your account.
If you have any queries on this matter, please do not hesitate to contact me. Thank you for your cooperation.

Final demand – open
Following my emails of (dates) I must inform you that we have still not received payment for the outstanding sum of €4,500.
I wrote to you on (dates) regarding the balance of €12,600 on your account. I attach copies of both emails. This sum is now two months overdue. We are very concerned that the matter has not yet received your attention.

Final demand – action
Unless we receive payment within seven days, we shall have no alternative but to take legal action to recover the money.
In the meantime, your existing credit facilities have been suspended.

Complaints and apologies

Complaining (customer)

Open	I am writing … … in connection with my order FS690 which arrived this morning. … to complain about the quality of a product I bought from your website. … to complain about the poor service we received from your company. … to draw your attention to the negative attitude of some people in your customer services section.
Complaint	Our order dated 16 September clearly stated that we wanted 1,000 items, however you … The goods were faulty/damaged/in poor condition. There seems to be an error in the invoice/a misunderstanding. The equipment I ordered has still not been delivered, despite my phone call to you last week to say that it is needed urgently. The product I received was well below the standard I expected. To make matters worse, when I called your company your staff …
Request for action	Please replace the faulty goods as soon as possible. We must insist on an immediate replacement/full refund. Unless I receive the goods by the end of this week, I will have no choice but to cancel my order.
Close	I hope that you will deal with this matter promptly as it is causing me considerable inconvenience.

Apologising (supplier)

Open	I am writing in relation to your recent complaint.
Apologising	I was very concerned to learn about … Please accept my sincere apologies. I would like to apologise for the inconvenience you have suffered.
Denying responsibility	We appreciate that this has caused you considerable inconvenience, but we cannot accept any responsibility in this matter.
Promising action	Can you leave it with me? I'll look into the matter and get back to you tomorrow. I have looked into the matter and … I have spoken to the staff involved, and … We will send replacement items/give you a refund immediately. I can assure you that this will not happen again. We're having a temporary problem with … . We're doing everything we can to sort it out.
Compensation	To compensate for the inconvenience, we would like to offer you …
Close	Thank you for bringing this matter to my attention. Please accept my assurance that it will not happen again. Once again, I hope you will accept my apologies for the inconvenience caused. I very much hope you will continue to use our services in the future. If you have any further queries, please do not hesitate to contact me on my direct line …

Personal

Being friendly

You heard something, but are not sure	It seems that … Apparently, …
Something is true, but surprising	Actually, … In fact, …
Something is obvious or already known	Obviously, … Of course, …
Good/bad fortune	Unfortunately, … Luckily, …
Saying what you really think	To be honest, … Frankly, …
Going back to a topic	Well, … So, … Anyway, …
Changing the topic	Anyway, … So, … By the way, …
Summarising with the most important point	Anyway, … Basically, …

Asking for advice

	Formal/Neutral	Informal
Open	I'd like your advice about a problem I have.	I've got a bit of a problem.
Asking for advice	I was wondering if you had any ideas about …? What would you advise me to do?	Do you have any ideas about …? What should I do?
Close	Please write back when you have the time and let me know what you think.	Please email me when you get the chance.

Giving advice

	Formal/Neutral	Informal
Open	I was sorry to hear about your current difficulties.	I'm sorry you're having such a hard time at the moment.
Giving advice	I think it might be a good idea to … Have you thought of … (+ -ing)?	I think you should … What about … (+ -ing)?
Result	This would mean that …	That way, …
Options	I think this option would be preferable to … (+ -ing)	I think it's better than … (+ -ing)
Close	I hope I have been of some help.	I hope I've helped a bit.

Suggestions

Making a suggestion	I think we should/I suggest that we/ Let's *go* to … Shall we/Perhaps we could/Why don't we *go* to …? I suggest/How about *going* to …?
Accepting	It's a great idea! I think your idea would work really well. It might be worth trying.

Rejecting	I'm not so sure about your idea.
	It sounds like a good idea, but I don't think it would work in practice.
	It sounds like a good idea, but I can see one or two problems.

Special situations

| Thanks | Just a quick note to say many thanks for … |
| | I really appreciate everything that you have done. |

| Good luck | Good luck with … |
| | I would like to take this opportunity to wish you every success in the future. |

Congratulations	Many congratulations on your promotion/new job.
	I was delighted to hear the news about …
	Well done!

| Best wishes | Please give my best wishes/regards to … |

Bad news	I was so sorry to hear about …
	I was really sorry to hear you're not well. … Hope you feel better soon.
	If there's anything I can do to help, let me know.

Job application

| Greeting (formal) | Dear Sir/Madam |

| Reason for writing | With reference to your advertisement on the … website, I am interested in applying for the post of … |

| Your background and experience | I am 26 years old and am currently studying for a degree in … at … University. |
| | For the last two months/years I have been working as a … at … . |

| The job itself | I am interested in this job because … |
| | I feel that I would be well-suited for this job as I enjoy/have a lot of experience in … . |

| Refering to your CV | I have attached my CV as a Word document. You will notice that I … as well as … . You will also notice that … . |

Final comments	I would be grateful if you would consider my application.
	You will see from my CV that two people can be contacted as references, one is … and the other is from … .
	I am available for interview in …/by phone any weekday afternoon, and you can email me or telephone me on the number below.

| Close | I look forward to hearing from you soon. |
| | Yours faithfully |

Reports

Report structure

Introduction / Background	As requested at the Board meeting of 18 April, here is my report.
	The report will discuss/consider/describe/analyse/review …
	The report is based on …
	I have divided the report into three sections.
Findings	The findings/figures/results/investigations show that …
	It appears that … . This has led to a situation where …
	The graph/table shows that …
Signposts	As can be seen in table 1/section 2/figure 3, …
	As mentioned above, …/…, see below.
	… and I will discuss this in more detail below/in section 3.2.
Conclusion / Recommendations	I (would like to) suggest/recommend that …
	My specific recommendations are as follows.
Closing comments	Please have a look at the report and let me have your comments.
	Please feel free to contact me if you have any questions.

Linking words

Sequence	Firstly, … Secondly, … Finally, …
Talking generally	In general, … Usually, … On the whole, …
Contrast	However, … Nevertheless, … On the other hand, …
Adding another point	In addition, … Moreover, … On another point, …
Examples	For example, … For instance, … e.g.
Alternatives	Either … or … Alternatively, … Instead of …
Real (surprising) situation	In fact, … Actually, … As a matter of fact, …
Something is obvious	Clearly, … Obviously, … Of course, …
Most important point	Especially, … Above all, … In particular, …
Rephrasing	In other words, … That is to say, … i.e.
Result/consequence	As a result, … Therefore, … For this reason, …
New topic	In relation to … Regarding … With reference to …

Careful, balanced style

Giving both sides of an argument	In general …, however …	On the whole …, but …
Making a statement less general	Many/Some …	Usually/Typically/Often …
Making a statement less certain	It is possible/probable that …	It seems/appears that … … tends to be …
Making a comparison less strong	substantially/considerably/much (+ comparative adjective)	
	significantly/relatively (+ comparative adjective)	
	marginally/slightly (+ comparative adjective)	
Concluding	On balance, …	
	Taking all the above points into consideration, …	

Answer key

Introduction

1 Formal or informal?

A

1 d 2 h 3 i 4 n 5 b 6 e 7 c 8 f 9 m 10 j 11 o
12 k 13 l 14 a 15 g

B

Email 1

Sorry, I can't make it on Friday. As I'll miss the meeting, could you send me a copy of the minutes? I'll write to Anita as well, to tell her (that) I won't be there. Once again, I'm sorry for this, and I promise (that) I'll be at the next meeting.

Email 2

Thanks for the email of 25 Jan where you asked for help on how to order on-line. I need to know your a/c number before I can deal with this. Please could you also provide details of which version of Windows you're using.

Email 3

Re your order number J891 – we received it this morning, but you haven't filled in the sections on size and colour. What exactly do you need? These products are selling very well at the moment, and I'm sorry to tell you that the medium size is temporarily out of stock. But we're expecting more supplies soon. Shall I email you when they arrive?

C

1 k 2 c 3 a 4 m 5 o 6 f 7 h 8 l 9 j 10 i 11 g
12 b 13 n 14 d 15 e

2 Missing words and abbreviations

A

1 c, j 2 b, i 3 e, f 4 a, d, k 5 h, l 6 g

B

It was a great evening wasn't it! I really enjoyed the meal, and it was nice to see Mary and Roger again. Have you had a chance to speak to Lucy yet? Don't worry if you haven't, I will be seeing her tomorrow.
About next week – the film you suggested sounds great. I've been talking to some colleagues at work about it. I'm not sure about the day, though. Tuesday might be difficult. Perhaps Wednesday would be better? Let me know.
I'm going to my parents at the weekend – I'm looking forward to it. They live in Chichester. Have you ever been there?
Sometime soon we need to talk about holiday plans for next summer. Things are still a bit uncertain at my work. It might be possible to take two weeks off in July, but I can't be sure. Three weeks would be impossible. It's a pity. Anyway, I've got to go now. I hope you're well. I'll see you next week.

C

1 b 2 a 3 d 4 c

D

Email 1

Subject: *Your order reference number KD654*
In relation to your order received today, we cannot supply the quantities you need at this moment. Please confirm as soon as possible if a part-delivery would be acceptable, with the rest to follow later. Regards, Stefan

Email 2

Subject: Thanks for your message
Regarding your message left on my answering machine – yes, I'm free for lunch on Wednesday next week. By the way, good news about your interview. Have to work now. See you, Jane.

Email 3

Subject: Options for Technical Help
We have a Technical Assistance section on our website, with an extensive list of Frequently Asked Questions. Customers find this very convenient as it is available 24 hours per/a day, 7 days a week. On the other hand, if you need to speak to somebody in person, you can call during working hours. Best wishes, Alan.

3 Key phrases

A

Email 1 Meeting 14/5
Email 2 Regarding your order
Email 3 Action re contract
Email 4 Special Offer!
Email 5 Shipping confirmation

B

1 *Re your last email*
2 Just a short note to let you know that …
3 Good news!
4 We can confirm that …
5 Sorry for …
6 Unfortunately, …
7 Please … / Can you …?
8 Can you …? / Please …?
9 Do you want me to …?
10 Shall I …?
11 I'll get back to you.
12 I've attached …
13 Thanks for your help.
14 If there's anything else, just let us know.
15 Looking forward to …
16 Regards / Best wishes
• more formal

Basics

4 Opening and closing

A

1 c 2 g 3 b 4 h 5 d 6 f 7 a 8 e

B

1–5d 2–1c 3–7a 4–4h 5–8e 6–6f 7–2g 8–3b

C

1 *Beg/Neut*		7 Beg/Neut
2 End/Inf		8 End/Inf
3 End/Neut		9 Beg/Neut
4 Beg/Inf		10 End/Neut
5 End/Inf		11 Beg/Inf
6 End/Neut		12 Beg/Inf

D

a) 3, 9   b) 1, 6, 7, 10   c) 4, 5, 8, 11, 12   d) 2

5 Giving news

A

1 formal   2 informal   3 informal   4 formal

B

1 I'm writing to confirm our appointment on Tuesday 6 June.
2 Unfortunately, I will not be able to make the meeting on Tuesday 6 June.
3 You will be pleased to hear that your application has been accepted.
4 We regret to inform you that your application has not been successful.
5 Bad news I'm afraid about our trip next weekend. / Bad news about our trip next weekend, I'm afraid.
6 You'll never guess what's happened!
7 Here's an update on the project.

C

a) 5, 6   b) 1, 2   c) 3, 4   d) 7

D

1 *Further*		5 reference
2 confirm/say		6 let
3 make/attend		7 Unfortunately
4 forward		8 attached

E

1 b 2 a 3 d 4 e 5 c 6 f

F

1 D 2 B 3 C 4 C 5 B 6 A 7 D 8 A 9 D 10 A
11 C 12 C 13 D 14 B

6 Information, action, help

A

1 seen/read
2 Please
3 Can/Could
4 trouble/co-operation/help
5 hearing
6 Regards/Yours
7 about/regarding
8 attached
9 require/need/want
10 hesitate

B

1 b 2 c 3 a 4 f 5 d 6 e 7 h 8 j 9 i 10 g

C

1 I'd like to know a little more about
2 I'd appreciate your help on this
3 Please get back to me if you need any more information
4 I'd like you to prepare a report
5 I need you to be there at the meeting
6 I'll send it to you
7 Can I ask you to look after them
8 Of course, I'd be pleased to help
9 Shall I show them round
10 Let me know if there's anything else

D

1 *I'd like to know a little more about …*
2 Please get back to me if you need any more information.
3 I'd appreciate your help on this.
4 I need you to …
5 I'd like you to … (Could you …)
6 Shall I …?
7 I'd really appreciate it.
8 Can I ask you to …?
9 Let me know if …
10 Of course.

7 Internal messages

A

Version 1 is not appropriate for an internal company communication. It is too long, and it is not clear what action the reader should take. Version 2 is better because it is easy to understand and has a clear structure.

B

Situation: Mr Bianchi of Ferrara Textiles will be looking around the company tomorrow, from about 12.00.
Objective: It is important to make a good impression.
Strategy: Please:
1 Inform all staff in your department.
2 Remind them to greet Mr Bianchi by name and take time to answer his questions.
3 Arrange lunch breaks so that there is always someone available in your section.
Closing comment: Thank you for your cooperation.

C

Model answer:
Subject: training course
I have found some information about a computer training course. I think it would be useful for someone from our department to attend. The details are as follows:
Course: Spreadsheets for Financial Planning.
Dates: 4 June – 8 June

Times: 18.00 – 19.30 every evening

Cost: €750

I am free and would like to go. Would it be possible for the company to pay?

Thank you.

D

Model answer:

Subject: Mrs Rothe's retirement

As you may know, Mrs Rothe will be retiring at the end of the year. She has been with the company for 15 years.

We would like to organise a leaving party for her, and present her with a small gift. Claudia will be coming round if you want to make a contribution.

The party will be after work on 20 December, in the main conference room. Everyone is welcome.

8 Attachments

A

1 *B, C* ('enclosed' is the word used when something is inside an envelope, but some people still use it for email)
2 A, D
3 B, D
4 A, B
5 A, C
6 B, C
7 C, D
8 B, C
9 A, B
10 A, D

B

1 hope you like <u>it</u>
2 return them <u>to</u> me
3 <u>I'm</u> sending
4 I have <u>attached</u>
5 you'll be <u>able</u> to
6 <u>carefully</u>
7 I <u>would</u> be grateful
8 forgot <u>to</u> send
9 <u>as</u> promised
10 what <u>do</u> you think
11 <u>I'll</u> let you know
12 <u>in</u> red

C

Email 1

1 find   2 Hope   3 Let

Email 2

4 sending/attaching   5 attention   6 by

Email 3

7 As   8 else/more   9 end

Email 4

10 forgot   11 Here   12 back

Email 5

13 would   14 could   15 note

9 Arranging a meeting

A

1 *be convenient*
2 one time
3 at, on, on
4 shall
5 return to
6 for, could be
7 occupied
8 Pardon me, control
9 a promise
10 What if, in place of
11 matter, away
12 regret again
13 see
14 telephone
15 compliments

B

1 on/next/–	8 How/What
2 in	9 instead
3 convenient/good/okay	10 able
4 regards	11 would
5 afraid/sorry	12 seeing/meeting
6 make/manage	13 call/ring
7 away/busy	14 any

C

1 b   2 e   3 d   4 a   5 f   6 c

D

1 are we still okay for Tuesday?
2 I need to finalise arrangements today.
3 can we reschedule for the following week?
4 something urgent has come up.
5 I'll circulate the agenda in the next few days.
6 let me know if you want to make any changes.

E

1 're *going*	6 'll take
2 're catching	7 're not doing/aren't doing
3 will be	8 'll have
4 're staying	9 are sending (will send)
5 're meeting	10 'll give

10 Invitations and directions

A

Formal company

Email 1

1 Dear Mary
2 We would be very pleased if you could come
3 It has been arranged
4 in order to
5 Your attendance will be very welcome.
6 it will not be necessary to
7 Refreshments will be provided
8 Your presence at the meeting will be very useful.
9 will be able to attend,

10 as soon as possible.
11 John Saunders

Email 2
12 Thank you for your kind invitation.
13 I would be delighted to attend
14 I am sure it will be very useful.
15 Would it be possible
16 Thank you once more for your invitation
17 I look forward to seeing you

Email 3
18 Thank you for your kind invitation.
19 Please accept my apologies.
20 let me have a copy of any report arising from the discussion.
21 we will have the opportunity to meet on another occasion in the near future.
22 I am sure that the meeting will be a great success.

Informal company
Email 1
1 Hi Mary
2 I'm writing to invite you
3 I've arranged it
4 to
5 It'd be great to see you.
6 you won't need to
7 There'll be plenty to eat and drink
8 Hope to see you in May!
9 can make it,
10 asap.
11 Stephanie

Email 2
12 Thanks a lot for the invite.
13 I'd love to come to
14 It sounds like a great idea.
15 Will it be okay
16 Thanks again,
17 see you

Email 3
18 Thanks a lot for the invite.
19 I'm very sorry that I will miss the meeting.
20 email me and let me know how it went.
21 we can meet up soon.
22 Good luck with the meeting!

B
1 would, could
2 presence/attendance, useful/welcome, make
3 let, know, as
4 kind, delighted/pleased, seeing/meeting
5 Unfortunately, appointment/meeting/commitment, apologies
6 opportunity/chance, near, success.

C
1 c 2 b 3 e 4 f 5 a 6 d

D
1 get/come	11 give
2 find	12 lost
3 by	13 do
4 turn	14 Either
5 on	15 country/countryside/park
6 until	16 yet
7 miss	17 feeling
8 past/by	18 stay
9 at	19 looking
10 in	20 wishes/regards

11 Negotiating a project

A
1 *Can*	8 could
2 would, could	9 should
3 could	10 might
4 need to	11 would
5 should	12 need to have
6 would	13 would
7 would	14 couldn't

B
1 c 2 f 3 i 4 d 5 h 6 b 7 g 8 j 9 a 10 e

C
1 What are your usual charges/rates for
2 How do you think we should deal with this?
3 Why don't you
4 My main concern at this stage is
5 Do you think you could
6 I'll be in touch again soon with more details.
7 We would be prepared to
8 I understand what you're saying about
9 Okay, I'm happy with that for now.
10 I look forward to working with you.

12 Checking understanding

A
1 the attachment
2 you mean
3 Which conference/one
4 me know
5 you sure/certain
6 open it
7 be wrong
8 to you

B
1 in on
2 back to

C
1 Sorry, you forgot to send the attachment. Can you send it again?

2 Did you mean to send this? I don't want to open the attachment in case it's got a virus.

3 Are you sure about that? I thought the conference was in Istanbul.

4 I'll check and get back to you later today.

5 Which conference do you mean?

6 Sorry, I don't understand this point. Can you explain it in a little more detail?

7 I'm not sure what you mean by this. Could you clarify?

8 I thought the meeting was on Thursday, but I may be wrong.

9 Sorry, forget my last email. You're right. It should be Thursday, not Friday.

10 What I meant was Gatwick, not Heathrow. I hope this clarifies the situation.

D

1 attached	7 point/term/word
2 Let	8 detail
3 forgot	9 latest
4 again	10 back
5 by	11 in
6 checked	12 wrong

Language focus

13 Verb forms

A

1 b) *present simple*
2 d) present continuous
3 f) present perfect
4 c) present perfect continuous
5 a) past simple
6 e) past continuous

B

Present simple
always/often/never; every day; from time to time; now; nowadays; once a year; these days

Present continuous
at the moment; currently; now; nowadays; these days

Present perfect
already; always/often/never; ever; just; not yet; over the last few months; recently; so far this year; up to now

Past simple
ago; always/often/never; every day; from time to time; in the nineties; last week; yesterday

C

1 interview
2 'm planning
3 need
4 've always been able to
5 're operating
6 have fallen
7 means
8 hope

D

1 've just received	5 distributed
2 need	6 want
3 've given out	7 've already contacted
4 had	8 think

E

1 haven't been	5 didn't recognise
2 met	6 was wearing
3 was waiting	7 has dyed
4 was	8 was going out

F

1 've been phoning	5 've been dieting
2 've been waiting	6 've started
3 Have you found	7 've been going
4 've decided	8 Have you ever done

14 Comparisons

A

1 *the fastest*
2 the biggest
3 easier, the easiest
4 less, the least
5 worse, the worst
6 further, the furthest
7 than
8 much
9 a little
10 one of our best
11 more than
12 more and more
13 better, the more
14 the best, ever
15 compared to/in comparison with
16 as expensive as
17 the same as
18 as many
19 as much
20 like

B

1 to	6 more and more
2 rainier	7 as
3 much	8 more expensive
4 friendliest	9 as
5 ever	10 more

C

1 *like*	8 much
2 best	9 same
3 the	10 more
4 to	11 as
5 less	12 with/to
6 compared	13 ever
7 than	14 more/further

D

1a) *a lot more than 50%*
1b) considerably more than 50%
2a) a little over 50%
2b) slightly more than 50%
3a) around 50%
3b) roughly 50%
4a) almost 50%
4b) nearly 50%
5a) far less than 50%
5b) much less than 50%

E

1 *little over*
2 much less than
3 around
4 nearly
5 slightly more than
6 roughly the same as

15 Sentence structure

A

1 You may remember me. We exchanged business cards at the Trade Fair last week.
2 Our advertising campaign is going well. We should consider extending it until June.
3 I am writing to ask about availability of rooms in July. I need a single room for 3 nights.
4 I am going to my parents next weekend. I haven't seen them for a long time.

B

1 I am writing from Head Office in Munich to let you know that I am coming to visit your offices in Moscow next month.
2 This will be part of a visit that I am making to all our subsidiaries in Central Europe.
3 I will take the opportunity to consult with you about our strategic plan for Central Europe, which we have been working on for some time.
4 I would also like to visit our production facility while I am in Moscow, and if there is time, some of the local suppliers as well.
5 I will contact you again as soon as I know the exact dates when I can travel.

C

Email 1

I am writing to thank you for your hospitality during my recent trip to Paris. The meetings were very productive, and I am sure that they lay the basis for a good long-term business relationship.

As well as the business side of things, I really appreciated the time you took to show me Notre Dame, and the wonderful meal that we had afterwards. The next time that you are in Munich it will be my pleasure to return your kindness.

Please give my regards to your colleagues in the Paris office, it was a great pleasure to meet them all.

Email 2

Thank you for taking the time to attend an interview with us last week. Unfortunately, we have to inform you that your application has not been successful.

As we mentioned in the interview, we had many applicants for this position and the standard of candidates was very high. While we were impressed with your interview, we did not feel that you have the necessary skills and experience for the position.

We appreciate your interest in working with us, and we would like to take this opportunity to wish you every success in the future.

16 Common mistakes

A

1 *I am writing*
2 ~~until~~ by Friday
3 ~~I will be~~ I would be
4 ~~attach~~ attached
5 ~~can to meet~~ can meet
6 ~~so soon as~~ as soon as
7 ~~I been~~ I've been
8 ~~more better~~ better/much better
9 ~~at 8 Feb~~ on 8 Feb
10 ~~don't can help~~ can't help
11 ~~informations~~ information
12 ~~to meet~~ to meeting
13 ~~I am really~~ I really
14 ~~the follow~~ the following
15 ~~I'm afraid but we~~ I'm afraid (that) we

B

1 reference <u>to</u> your
2 you <u>for</u> sending
3 inform <u>you</u> that
4 able <u>to</u> confirm
5 apologise <u>for</u> the
6 appreciate <u>it</u> if
7 get back <u>to</u> me
8 would <u>be</u> convenient
9 you <u>would</u> like
10 think <u>I'll</u> stop
11 meet you <u>at</u> the
12 hearing <u>from</u> you
13 a copy <u>of</u> the
14 invitation <u>to</u> visit
15 reference <u>to</u> your

C

Email 1, first paragraph

~~going visit~~ *going to visit* / ~~I like to~~ I would like to / ~~to showing you~~ to show you

Email 1, second paragraph

~~would being~~ would be / ~~Please to let~~ Please let / ~~to see you~~ to seeing you

Email 2, first paragraph

~~we been interviewing~~ we have been interviewing / ~~to inform that~~ to inform you that / ~~member of team~~ member of the team

Email 2, second paragraph

~~invite you a short~~ invite you to a short / ~~have chance~~ have a chance / ~~can to estimate~~ can estimate

Email 3, first paragraph

~~I am write~~ I am writing / ~~was transfer~~ was transferred / ~~we yet haven't~~ we still haven't (we haven't received the goods yet)

Email 3, second paragraph

~~told~~ said (told me) / ~~at the morning~~ in the morning / ~~for to lose~~ to lose

Email 4, first paragraph

~~not so good as~~ not as good as / ~~remember you~~ remind you / ~~particular~~ particularly (in particular)

Email 4, second paragraph

~~I could be grateful~~ I would be grateful / ~~at the later~~ at the latest / ~~I also~~ I'll also

17 Punctuation and spelling

A

Dear Antoine Curiel

I am the Sales Manager for Genetech, a small biotechnology company based in Cologne. I attended your presentation at the Eurotech conference in Paris in November and we met briefly afterwards. Here is the information I said I would send, including our latest annual report. I hope it is of interest.

Best regards

Michael Bretz

B

Hi Jean – how are you? Thanks for your email about Mr Williams. In fact, I'm meeting him on Friday 16 March. We're meeting in his Brussels office and I'm a bit nervous about it because I don't speak French very well! He's the Marketing Director of the company, and reports directly to the CEO. It's going to be an interesting meeting, and I haven't been to Belgium before, so I'm looking forward to it. Anyway, I'll be in touch when I get back.

C

Angela – have you read John's report yet? I think its main conclusions are correct. This is basically what he's saying: sales are flat, and have been so for months; there's no new products in the pipeline, despite our large R&D budget; and our share price is at its lowest point since last November. I hope the Board take it seriously.

D

1 *which*	13 accommodation
2 received	14 cities
3 haven't	15 beginning
4 replied	16 February
5 really	17 it's
6 Actually	18 great
7 finally	19 completely
8 successful	20 different
9 independent	21 restaurant
10 interesting	22 opportunity
11 arrangements	23 Hopefully
12 their	24 people

25 responsibilities	28 visiting
26 money	29 England
27 could	30 forward

Commercial

18 A customer–supplier sequence

A

1 d 2 c 3 e 4 b 5 a

6 1/4/5   7 2/3

B

1 *an inquiry*	5 an order
2 information	6 an invoice (with the goods)
3 a quotation	7 a complaint
4 the quotation	8 the problem

C

1 *b* 2 a 3 f 4 d 5 c 6 h 7 e 8 g

D

1 *supply*	5 standard
2 advertisement	6 terms
3 acknowledge receipt of	7 willing
4 value for money	8 charges

19 Inquiries and orders

A

a) *Inquiry 2*	f) Reply 3
b) Reply 2	g) Inquiry 3
c) Inquiry 5	h) Inquiry 1
d) Inquiry 4	i) Reply 5
e) Reply 1	j) Reply 4

B

1 c 2 a 3 e 4 b 5 d

6 b 7 e 8 d 9 c 10 a

C

1 *attached, delay*	7 accept, quotation
2 would, grateful	8 processed, track
3 first-time, pre-payment	9 note, records
4 discount, repeat	10 temporarily, stock
5 dispatched, firm	11 apologise, inconvenience
6 assure, prompt	12 correct, amend

20 Discussing and agreeing terms

A

1 d 2 g 3 e 4 a 5 c 6 h 7 b 8 f

9 an order   10 an offer   11 an agreement   12 a compromise

B

Email 1

1 *list*	7 credit
2 units	8 terms
3 order	9 guarantee
4 discounts	10 latest
5 size	11 reach
6 prepared	12 well-known

Email 2

13 relation
14 regard/reference
15 first-time
16 compromise
17 control
18 procedure
19 full/further
20 stock
21 place
22 fill
23 team
24 deal

C

1	for	10	to
2	in	11	of
3	on	12	for
4	with	13	ahead
5	on	14	in
6	by	15	on
7	on	16	over
8	on	17	from
9	for	18	within

21 Asking for payment

A

1 *I wish to draw your attention to my two previous emails.*
2 There is an overdue payment on your account.
3 We are concerned that the matter has not yet received your attention.
4 This situation cannot be allowed to continue.
5 We must urge you to take immediate action to settle your account.
6 We have still not received payment for the outstanding sum.
7 We shall have no alternative but to take legal action to recover the money.
8 We would appreciate your cooperation in resolving this matter.

B

First reminder: email 3
Second reminder: email 4
Third reminder: email 2
Final demand: email 1

C

1 a   2 b   3 a   4 b

D

1 concerning a payment
2 should have been cleared
3 to settle your account
4 have still not received
5 the outstanding sum
6 further delay
7 now two months overdue
8 forward the payment
9 shall have no alternative

22 Describing business trends

A

1 a) *go down*   e) decrease
  b) fall   f) shrink
  c) get worse   g) be down
  d) hit a low   h) be stable

2 *go–went–gone*
  rise–rose–risen
  grow–grew–grown
  fall–fell–fallen

3 a) *slowly*
  b) sharply
  c) slightly
  d) gradually
  e) significantly
  f) steadily

4 a gradual improvement, slow growth

5 a) by
  b) of
  c) in
  d) from, to, by
  e) since, for

B

1	at	5	figures	9	for
2	rose	6	by	10	at
3	to	7	steady	11	rapidly
4	of	8	growth	12	watch

C

1 *I'm sure*
2 won't
3 I expect
4 probably won't
5 are likely to
6 I doubt
7 could
8 may not (might not)
9 might
10 might not (may not)
(*NOT* used: won't probably, could not)
11 c   12 a   13 b

D

1 likely
2 at
3 will increase
4 uncertain
5 will probably
6 to raise interest rates
7 likely to
8 considerably
9 increasing
10 might have
11 probably won't
12 it's going to rain

23 Cause, effect, contrast

A

1 to, in
2 therefore, as
3 from, of, of, to
4 because, due

B

1 such
2 as a result
3 so
4 due to
5 led to
6 because
7 So
8 because of

C

1 *though*, although
2 whereas, while
3 spite, despite
4 spite, Despite
5 fact that
6 However, Nevertheless, Even
7 though
8 Even

D

1 D 2 B 3 C 4 D 5 C 6 A 7 C 8 D 9 A 10 B
11 A 12 C 13 A 14 D

Problems

24 Complaints

A

1 connection, attitude
2 matter, inconvenience
3 delivered, urgently
4 purchased, standard
5 attention, problem
6 appreciate, replaced
7 terms, treatment
8 entitled, replacement
9 dissatisfaction, received
10 unless, cancel
11 complain, quality
12 refund, further

B

1 f 2 g 3 a 4 c 5 b 6 h 7 e 8 d

C

1 *connection*
2 urgently
3 further
4 refund
5 attention
6 standard
7 terms
8 dissatisfaction
9 replacement
10 inconvenience

D

1 *Furthermore*, In addition
2 Finally, Firstly
3 However, Nevertheless
4 Even though, In spite of the fact that
5 As a result, Therefore
6 Above all, In particular
7 In fact, In reality
8 In conclusion, Taking everything into consideration
• Even though, In spite of the fact that

E

1 *Firstly*
2 However
3 Furthermore
4 Above all

5 In fact
6 in spite of the fact that
7 As a result
8 Taking everything into consideration

25 Apologies

A

Email 1

1 *on behalf of*
2 unprofessional conduct
3 Please accept my sincere apologies for
4 You have my assurance that
5 resolve the matter to your satisfaction
6 We will
7 To compensate for the inconvenience caused
8 regarding the incident
9 If you have any further queries
10 do not hesitate to contact me

Email 2

11 for
12 unfortunate behaviour
13 I'm really sorry for
14 You can be sure that
15 sort out the problem
16 I'll
17 As a friendly gesture
18 about what happened
19 If there's anything else
10 please call

B

1 g 2 j 3 f 4 i 5 b 6 a 7 c 8 h 9 d 10 e

C

1 ~~absolutely~~
2 ~~material~~
3 ~~wares~~
4 ~~out of work~~
5 ~~an inflammation in our warehouse~~
6 ~~sort out it~~
7 ~~restore them~~
8 ~~disadvantage~~

D

1 Thank you very much for bringing this matter to my attention.
2 I was very concerned to learn about the problems you experienced.
3 I will look into the matter and get back to you within the next few days.
4 Once again, please accept our apologies for the inconvenience caused.
5 Having looked into this matter in detail, I regret that I can be of no further assistance.

Reports

26 Report structure and key phrases

A

1 b   2 d   3 a   4 e   5 c

B

1 f   2 d   3 a   4 e   5 c   6 b   7 k   8 j   9 h   10 g   11 l
12 i

Introduction/Background: 1, 2, 3, 4

Findings: 5, 6, 7

Conclusion/Recommendations: 8, 9

Closing comments: 10, 11, 12

C

1 purpose of the report
2 based on the figures
3 divided the report
4 can be seen
5 led to a situation
6 above
7 shows that
8 See section 4.2
9 I suggest that
10 as follows
11 make reductions
12 investigate the possibility
13 identify opportunities
14 let me have

27 Linking words and relative clauses

A

1 *In general,* However, in addition, As a result,
2 In relation to, so, Nevertheless, Obviously, On another point, as,
3 In particular,
4 Firstly, Secondly, In fact, So, that is to say, Alternatively, especially

B

1 *Secondly, Finally*
2 On the whole, Usually
3 Nevertheless, On the other hand
4 Moreover, On another point
5 e.g., For instance
6 Alternatively, Instead of
7 Actually, As a matter of fact
8 Obviously, Of course
9 Above all, In particular
10 i.e., That is to say
11 For this reason, Therefore
12 Regarding, With reference to

C

1 The report *that the Board issued describes options for our long-term strategy.*
2 The Board *issued a report which describes options for our long-term strategy.*

3 We interviewed three candidates who were all very good.
4 The three candidates that we interviewed were all very good.
5 Marketing want to postpone the product launch, which I feel is a mistake.
6 The workers who we might need to dismiss are listed below.
7 The team whose results were particularly good should be given a bonus.

Direct/Indirect

28 Being direct and brief

A

1 Version 2
2 Version 1
3 Version 1
4 Version 2
5 Version 2
6 Version 1

B

Model answer:

Subject: Meeting 7 Feb

Re our phone call, the meeting place you suggested is fine – lobby of the Intercontinental Hotel in Barcelona, 2.00 on 7 Feb. Look forward to seeing you there. Please be my guest for dinner in the evening.

C

Many thanks for your email ~~which I received yesterday~~. Tuesday at 10.30 is fine for me ~~as my 9am meeting will be finished by then~~. Can you send me the latest sales figures before the meeting? ~~I look forward to seeing you there~~.

D

~~I am writing to all my colleagues to let you know that~~ I will be away from my office from 14–21 November ~~on a visit to Hungary~~. Please direct all questions ~~that you have~~ to Helga in my absence.

E

Model answer:

Subject: Baltic States

Thanks for sending me the info about the Baltic States – it was really useful. I've forwarded your email to our representative in Estonia, Krista Kilvet. Would you be interested in giving a presentation at Head Office on the political and economic background in the region? I'm sure the Board would be interested.

F

Model answer:

Subject: Thank you for your help

Thank you for all your help during the conference in London last week. It was really appreciated. Please give my best regards to all your UK sales team – it was a great pleasure to meet them. I look forward to seeing you in Dubai at the end of the year.

29 Being indirect and polite

A

1 *Could you possibly* / I was wondering if you could
2 Is it all right if I / I wonder if I could
3 Do you need any help with / Would you like me to
4 Perhaps we should / Why don't we

B

1 *afraid*, small	5 Actually, doesn't, much
2 seems, slight	6 Wouldn't
3 think, may	7 might, quite
4 honest, sure	8 won't, cheap

C

1 I wonder (was wondering) if we could meet again next week?
2 There seems to be a mistake on the invoice.
3 The quality is not very high.
4 Would you like me to speak to Mr Baker?
5 Your estimate for the cost might be a bit low.
6 Wouldn't it be a better idea to wait?
7 To be honest, I'm not sure it's a good idea.
8 Perhaps we should think about cancelling the project.

D

1 *sounds*, practice
2 saying, what about
3 Wouldn't, little
4 honest, sure, convenient
5 mean
6 don't, would, better
a) 1, 2, 5, 6   b) 2   c) 3, 6   d) 4

E

1 It seems/I think it's
2 quite/a bit/a little/rather
3 Wouldn't it be
4 we haven't been very happy
5 a small favour
6 I was wondering if you could
7 It's a bit delicate
8 I might/may be
9 (To be honest) I'm not sure (that) I agree
10 seem/seems to be/might be
11 quite/a bit/a little/too
12 would

Personal

30 Being friendly

A

1 Apparently	5 Frankly
2 In fact	6 Anyway
3 Of course	7 By the way
4 Luckily	8 Basically

B

1 Actually/In fact/To be honest
2 Luckily
3 Anyway/Well/So
4 Unfortunately
5 By the way/Anyway/So/Well
6 Apparently/It seems that/Well
7 To be honest/Frankly/Actually
8 Anyway/Basically/Of course/Obviously/Well

C

The email makes sense without the words underlined, but it is not very friendly. The extra words give a little more detail and interest, and they show your feelings and your personality.

D

Model answer:

Stefan, just a few lines to let you know that I can't join you next weekend. I'm really sorry because I'm sure you'll have great fun, but I've already arranged to go to Paris. I'm staying with Bernard in his flat, and to be honest I really need a break. Things have been a bit difficult recently. First, I've broken up with Rosanna, as you probably know. We've been having a lot of arguments recently, and she told me last month she is going to move to Hamburg. It's a pity, but I think it's best for both of us. Then, the next thing is my job. I have a lot of responsibilities in the office and it's quite stressful. We have hundreds of customers who call all day long and I never get a break. Oh well, that's life! I'm sorry if I sound a bit depressed, but writing to you has helped. Anyway, that's all for now. Hope to see you soon. All the best, Wilhelm.

31 Advice and suggestions

A

a) 3   b) 5   c) 2   d) 7   e) 1   f) 10   g) 9   h) 4   i) 8   j) 6

• In general phrases a)–j) are more formal, although some examples like b) and d) have a similar level of formality.

B

1 *you can*	5 it might
2 I should	6 you could
3 me know	7 be preferable
4 such a	8 I have

C

1 *a*   2 d   3 b   4 c   5 a/b   6 e   7 b   8 a
9 h   10 j   11 f   12 k   13 i   14 g

D

1 wondering, could
2 get/have, appreciate
3 should, better
4 about, might/could/would
5 Shall, about
6 work, worth

32 Job application

A

1 c   2 g   3 i   4 f   5 n   6 k   7 j   8 d   9 b   10 l   11 e
12 m   13 a   14 h

B

Dear Sir/Madam //

With reference to your advertisement on the JobFinders.com website, I am interested in applying for the post of tour leader for Italian school students. //

I am 26 years old and am currently studying for a diploma in Tourism at Naples University. After that I hope to follow a career in the travel industry. During the last few summer holidays I have worked as a youth leader in Italy, and I enjoyed the work very much. Next summer I would like to do something more varied and challenging, and for this reason I am interested in the job of tour leader, taking students to London. //

I feel that I would be well-suited for this job as I enjoy working with young people. I have a lot of energy and enthusiasm and am also responsible and reliable. //

I have attached my CV as a Word document. You will notice that I have supervised children on a range of sports and cultural activities as well as dealing with transport arrangements and tickets. You will also notice that my English is good and I have First Certificate grade A. //

I would be grateful if you would consider my application. You will see from my attached CV that two people can be contacted as references, one is a university professor and the other is from the summer programme where I worked last year. I am available for interview in Naples any weekday afternoon, and you can email me or telephone me on the number below. //

I look forward to hearing from you soon. //

Yours faithfully

C

1 to, on, in, for
2 as
3 for, in
4 as
5 on, in
6 to, from
7 of, at
8 at, of
9 for, in
10 in
11 for
12 as